"*Healing for Every Heart in Adoption* lives up to its title. The author
generously share their stories with
dom. In doing so, they offer permi
the complicated and beautiful expe
side them and invite them into the
Jamie Finn, founder, Foster

T0274592

..... L..L. r ulIIly

"This book is at once personal testimony and practical guidance,
aching confession and breathtaking faith, private prayer and invitation into prayerful fellowship with others who have walked
similar paths. Amid a culture that leans heavily on tips, techniques, and simplistic coinage, this book is a sturdy alternative.
It applies a profound and enduring approach centered in the un-
paralleled healing power to be found only in honesty, repentance,
forgiveness, and full release to the God who formed and loves us."
Jedd Medefind, president, Christian Alliance for Orphans,
and Rachel Medefind, director, CAFO Institute
for Family-Centered Healing & Health

"*Healing for Every Heart in Adoption* is a pioneering, breakthrough
must-read for every adoptive parent, adoptee, and birth parent.
It will bring comfort, educate, reveal the source of behavior, and
point to the greatest Father who longs to heal and restore. The
trio of authors brings power-packed revelation from their unique
perspectives."
Patricia Bootsma, pastor, Catch the Fire Ministries; global prayer
coordinator, JH Israel; author, *Raising Burning Hearts*
and *When Jesus Splits the Sky*

"These authors, who represent all three parts of the adoption
triad, have walked through incredibly painful experiences and
been transformed by the healing hand of God. They vulnerably
share their stories with hearts full of hope! You'll need to grab a
box of tissues and then pray the prayers at the end of each chapter. You will not be the same after reading this book."
Joyce Koo Dalrymple, founder/CEO, Refuge for Strength; author,
Women of the New Testament and *Jesus' Passion Week*

"Spoken directly from the heart into the hearts of everyone
touched by adoption. Every very real emotion and challenge that
you have experienced is gracefully and compassionately explored
in this book. You will feel seen, heard, and loved on every page."
Karla Marie Williams, global advocate for children
and families; speaker and author

"What a gem to find this sacred written space where the adoption
triad can be clearly heard—grief and all! This resource is rich in

experiences but, more that that, in a true acknowledgment of the complex dynamics of an adoption story impacted by the healing power of relationships rooted in the gospel."

Aixa de Lopez, board member, Alianza Cristiana para los Huérfanos

"Jesus came to heal the brokenhearted and to free those who are oppressed. With this in mind, this team of authors has put together a brilliant transparent book. Whether you are an adoptive or biological parent, child, or other family member, God has a purpose and plan for your life. Learn from experienced practitioners the healing and redemptive path as we each cry out 'Abba, Daddy, Father' to our Lord and Creator."

James W. Goll, God Encounters Ministries, GOLL Ideation LLC

"Who better to embrace the wounds of adoption than those who have walked the journey? Who better to celebrate the depth of healing than those who have experienced it? Lisa, Betsy, and Jodi, who all encountered God in their stories, present a meaningful guide for redemption to those touched by adoption. Their insights and transparency are infused with wisdom and faith. I love this book and highly recommend it!"

Jayne E. Schooler, Schooler Institute; coauthor, *Caring for Kids from Hard Places*

"This is a refreshingly honest and compassionate perspective in a world where the adoption narrative is often oversimplified. Beautifully and redemptively written, it acknowledges the complexities and brokenness that are experienced in the adoption journey. The heartfelt prayers, scriptural guidance, and deeply personal stories resonated with me across every page, and the raw truth and transformative power of Scripture is a beacon of hope for anyone experiencing the journey of adoption. This book is a must-read to navigate the path from brokenness to wholeness with faith as the anchor."

Pam Parish, founder and CEO, Connections Homes; author, *Ready or Not, Battle-Weary Parents, The Gift*, and *Redemptive Connection*

"As I read each chapter of this book, I was so moved by the raw stories that were told and the freedom prayers that were so carefully written. I could see myself, as an adoptive mom, in the pages. Hearing each perspective gave me new insight into my children and their birth families and tangible ways to pray for them. I look forward to sharing this book with everyone I know touched by adoption."

Kayla North, cofounder and CCO, One Big Happy Home; TBRI practitioner and MSOYW facilitator

HEALING FOR EVERY HEART IN ADOPTION

HEALING FOR EVERY HEART IN ADOPTION

Redemptive Prayers and Strategies for Adoptive
Parents, Adoptees, and Birth Parents

BETSY S. KYLSTRA, LISA C. QUALLS, AND JODI JACKSON TUCKER

Chosen

a division of Baker Publishing Group
Minneapolis, Minnesota

Published by Chosen Books
Minneapolis, Minnesota
ChosenBooks.com

Chosen Books is a division of
Baker Publishing Group, Grand Rapids, Michigan

Printed in the United States of America

Library of Congress Cataloging-in-Publication Data
Names: Kylstra, Betsy, author. | Qualls, Lisa, author. | Tucker, Jodi Jackson, author.
Title: Healing for every heart in adoption : redemptive prayers and strategies for adoptive parents, adoptees, and birth parents / Betsy S. Kylstra, Lisa C. Qualls, and Jodi Jackson Tucker.
Description: Minneapolis, Minnesota : Chosen Books, a division of Baker Publishing Group, [2024] | Includes bibliographical references.
Identifiers: LCCN 2024010326 | ISBN 9780800772888 (paper) | ISBN 9780800772895 (casebound) | ISBN 9781493448210 (ebook)
Subjects: LCSH: Adoption—Religious aspects—Christianity. | Adoptive parents—Prayers and devotions.
Classification: LCC HV875.26 .K59 2024 | DDC 362.7340973—dc23/eng/20240516
LC record available at https://lccn.loc.gov/2024010326

Cover design by Christopher Gilbert, Studio Gearbox

Baker Publishing Group publications use paper produced from sustainable forestry practices and postconsumer waste whenever possible.

24 25 26 27 28 29 30   7 6 5 4 3 2 1

FROM BETSY

To my husband, Chester, who has lovingly shared my healing journey for fifty years. Your help and passion to see God's transformation go beyond ourselves have shaped and enriched our lives together. To my children and their spouses—James and Chelsea, Lewis, Pam and Andrew, Eric and Nina—your loving support means the world to me. To my grandchildren—James Francis, Charlie Gray, Daily Finisterre, and Lewis Merritt—each of you makes my heart sing.

FROM LISA

To Russ. You have borne witness to my grief journey since we were seventeen. Together, we've experienced the Lord's redemptive and healing power. Your love, prayers, and steadfastness are a balm to my heart.

FROM JODI

To my beloved children. The richness of your love and the magnificence of your courage are the inspiration that fuels my day. I am who I am because of you. You are my treasures.

CONTENTS

FOREWORD

When I was ten years old, I ran away from an abusive home in Uganda. I decided that I'd rather be an orphan living on the streets and die at the hands of a stranger than to get killed by my own father. For five years I lived on the streets, doing whatever was needed to survive.

While trying to steal from a stranger, I met a man who changed my life. This stranger didn't see a street kid or a smelly teenager trying to rob him, but rather a young man with potential. He fed me for a year and a half until one day he said, "If you had the opportunity to go back to school, would you?" This man helped me to finish high school, and then supported my education at universities in Uganda and England. He brought me into his home, and I became a part of his family.

Because of my journey, I understand the struggle of those who have ended up separated from their biological parents. Even after we find a loving home, we still struggle with feelings of abandonment, rejection, shame, grief, loss, and much more. Some of us lash out in anger and rebellion. Others, like me, work really hard to avoid doing anything that would get us kicked out of the opportunity to be a part of a family.

When I went to university, I felt I didn't belong and that something was wrong with me. Even within a loving family that supported me, I felt I wasn't enough because I wasn't their biological child. I was overly sensitive, trying to do everything right, so much so that my health suffered under the stress of trying to be perfect.

I also understand the role of an adoptive parent. I have three adopted children, and in the last eight years I've fostered forty-one children as a single father. My story is unique, and so is yours. No matter what our journeys have been, we all must learn to deal with root issues that drive unhealthy behaviors. That's why this special book by Betsy, Lisa, and Jodi can be so helpful.

Because of the example of a dad from the man who rescued me, I wanted to be like him and help others like me. I knew, however, that I could not hold on to the trauma I had experienced growing up. I had to heal. I found my healing through faith in God and believing He had a purpose for my life. I have tried to be faithful to that purpose of helping other children who need a loving home.

This book can point you toward the healing you're looking for. You will find insight, understanding, and compassion for those in your adoption story, along with useful prayers that will help you heal from past hurts and wounds. There is hope ahead, so don't give up. The effort is worth it.

Peter Mutabazi, international advocate for children; founder, Now I Am Known; author, *Now I Am Known*

ONE

BEGINNING WITH HOPE

"I know the plans I have for you," declares the LORD, "plans to prosper you and not to harm you, plans to give you hope and a future." —Jeremiah 29:11

Hope does not disappoint us, because God's love has been poured into our hearts through the Holy Spirit that has been given to us. —Romans 5:5 NRSV

Welcome. We're proud of you, because you've taken the first step. You picked up this book, and you turned its first pages. You have the courage to heal. And the fullness of joy is waiting for you at the end of your journey.

Adoption is a beautiful thing, but it's also an experience riddled with challenges. We understand. We write as three people who together have known this journey in all its multiple facets. We've spent our lives in the story of adoption, and we've lived it from all its perspectives. We've also found a deep healing, and we want to share our stories of hope and joy with you.

In these pages you'll hear from an adoptive mother, a birth mother who became an adoptive mother, and an adoptee whose story birthed a healing ministry with global impact. We share deeply from our hearts, baring our souls to give you our best. Be gentle with us. We've made many mistakes, and we're still on the journey of living out this assignment. God is always teaching us, so don't be surprised if you know things we've not yet learned.

Our faith is what unites us deeply as authors. While our faith traditions and histories are different, we now each live our lives with our GPS pointed toward heaven. We believe in one God who reveals Himself to us as Father, Son (Jesus), and Holy Spirit.

All throughout the Bible are many references to God's adopting people into His family. We know we can learn from this and draw from the strength of the very One who has always had a heart for the abandoned one, always had a heart for the orphan. God is on your side. We are all adopted, grafted into His family.

These ideas may be new for you, but you'll find wisdom here. And even if your faith is unsure, you can still find insight and healing through these pages. So keep reading.

This book begins with the brokenness that led us all to the experience of adoption. But that's not the end of our stories. Healing is possible, and we've seen great miracles of healing and marvelous stories of redemption for all those involved in adoption. On these pages we'll walk through that journey from brokenness to restoration together.

To help you along this journey, Betsy has provided what we call Freedom Prayers. We encourage you to see these freedom-giving prayers as part of God's plan to redeem all that's been lost and heal all that's been broken. So please engage your heart as you pray them.

You'll find that some of the prayers are quite structured and specific (chapters 1–5) and others are more free-flowing (chapters 6–10). When we deal with specific areas of wounding, you'll see a prayer for each role: birth mother, adoptee, and adoptive parent. Otherwise, we have one prayer for everyone. Finally, the Freedom Prayers in the last two chapters (11 and 12) are unique as specific directions are provided within them.

All the Freedom Prayers, however, contain opportunities to repent, accept God's forgiveness, forgive yourself, forgive others, and release negative feelings and emotions to the Lord. The powerful spiritual prayer elements of repentance, forgiveness, and prayer all help address the spiritual roots of a problem.

Here's a word of explanation about each one:

Repent—a word and concept used throughout the Bible—may be familiar to you. It involves the confession of our wrongdoing (our sin), including wrong thoughts or attitudes. It involves a willingness to change our hearts. It means to turn around and go in a different direction than the old sinful pathway. Repentance is nontrivial. It's one of the major ways we must come back into a right relationship with the Lord.

> The powerful spiritual prayer elements of repentance, forgiveness, and prayer all help address the spiritual roots of a problem.

Forgive is next. Though never easy, it's essential—a main key to healing. When you choose to forgive someone or an organization, you give them a gift they don't deserve, just as the Lord gave you a gift you didn't deserve—His forgiveness. Forgiveness doesn't mean the wrong done to you was somehow okay. Not at all. Rather, it means you choose to let God be the judge of that person's or organization's wrongdoing, not you. You release the need to retaliate, to hurt back in return. Forgiveness also clears the slate for God's blessings to flow to you more abundantly. (You can look forward to chapter 10, where we share our stories about God's leading us through forgiveness.)

Last, we *release* our pain and negative emotions and give them to God. In many places in Scripture, we see that God's people poured out their troubles and pain to Him. We weren't designed to carry them. Over time, holding on to them leads to various ills. Keeping hate or fear or bitterness inside could be compared to drinking a poison potion and retaining it in our bodies.

One powerful illustration of releasing is found in Psalm 142 (NASB), where David pours out his heart to the Lord. He uses phrases like "I pour out my complaint before Him; I declare my trouble before Him" (verse 2); "In the way where I walk they have hidden a trap for me. Look to the right and see; for there is no one who regards me; there is no escape for me; no one cares for my soul" (verses 3–4); and "Deliver me from my persecutors, for they are too strong for me. Bring my soul out of prison" (verses 6–7). We can release our troubles in the same way.

Be assured that the Lord will not be burdened by taking your pain. But He can't carry it unless you give it up to Him.

Jesus desires us to give Him our pain. Isaiah 53 is a prophetic chapter about Jesus receiving it. It says He will carry our grief and our sorrows—all our mental and emotional pain (verses 4–5).

Be assured that the Lord will not be burdened by taking your pain. He's already carried it at the cross. But He can't carry it unless you give it up to Him, and that's the huge catch.

Friends often help, and talking with them brings true comfort. Jesus, however, can actually carry your pain. That's qualitatively different, and your life will change when releasing your pain to Him becomes your lifestyle.

Take advantage of all God wants to give you. Whether you're a young adult who was fostered or adopted, the parent of an adoptive family, or a birth parent who's lived with the heartache of loss, we know God has something for you in this book. And although we most often speak about and to women, we believe men who are part of an adoption story can also benefit from the healing principles we share.

Now, before we get started, we'll each tell you something about ourselves.

Betsy's Story

There I was, all six pounds of me, newly born in a Salvation Army shelter for expectant teenagers. The year was 1940. My birth mom, having just turned seventeen, would give me to an adoption agency and try to make a fresh start by moving to a new city. Within two months I would be placed in a wonderful home to join my four-year-old, also-adopted brother. Mine was a closed adoption, typical of that era.

I grew up in an almost ideal situation—in a small, safe town with stable, loving parents. My dad taught Bible at a small college, and my mom, a homemaker par excellence, was a pastor's daughter. Their faith was steadfast and winsome. They were balanced people, much loved in their community.

It's been said that some things are better caught than taught, and it was easy to catch my parents' faith. It was authentic and natural. One morning at family prayers, my father opened his eyes, looked at his watch, and ended the prayer rather abruptly. "Excuse us, Lord. The school bus is coming. We're about to be late." God was our friend, our anchor, the center of our family's life together.

I now recognize that if I—growing up in a loving, safe environment—still had such huge issues affecting my life, how much more difficult it may be for an adopted person growing up in a less loving and safe situation. This is particularly true if the adoption is cross-cultural or the child experienced multiple foster care placements before adoption. Although having some beautiful advantages, open adoptions may also leave the adopted child with two sets of parents and two different worldviews to navigate. This is also not easy.

Each of us adoptees has experienced a large measure of brokenness, perhaps even trauma. My personal adoption wounds often fought against my faith, and for years they won. I experienced times of failure, sinfulness, deadly loneliness, grief, shame, anger, and suicidal fantasies. Name it, and I've been there. Because of God's love, however—as well as loving parents and my birth mom's prayers—I was eventually healed and restored even though it was an uphill battle. God was there for me at every crucial crossroad of my life, showing me His heart for me and inviting me to live closer to Him.

In my thirties and forties, God not only healed me dramatically but released His principles of healing to both my husband and me. Once we were more healed, He put in us a tremendous desire to share His principles and healing with others. In the same time period, I was earning degrees in both secular and Christian counseling. I would eventually work as a counselor and minister and become an ordained minister. And my husband and I founded a healing ministry called Restoring The

Foundations International,[1] which eventually grew to establish bases in nineteen countries.

It's a privilege for me to share my adoption story and the healing of my wounds with you.

Lisa's Story

Adoption touched my life for the first time when I was a teen and got pregnant. Not knowing what to do, my parents turned to the church and were advised to send me to live in a foster home. I had a deep desire to parent my son, but the pressure on me to place him for adoption was relentless. I was completely alone with nobody to help me. Despite all my efforts, tears, and pleading, I had no option but to let go of my beautiful baby. This was a loss of such devastation that I didn't think I would survive.

My deepest sorrow led me to our beautiful Savior, Jesus. As I walked through my darkest valley, He surrounded me, and I began a lifelong relationship with Him. He redeemed my life and carried me through my grief. He also gave me a husband, Russ, who loved me and understood my sorrow. The Lord blessed us with seven incredible children, and my life was filled with love. To my great surprise, my son and I reconnected when he was sixteen. The cord between us had been stretched but never broken.

In 2006, the Lord opened my eyes to the orphan crisis in Ethiopia, and despite all my trauma and bitterness toward adoption, I felt drawn to the children who needed families. Russ and I loved being parents and having a big family, and we wanted to share what we had with children who had no parents to care for them.

In 2007, we adopted three unrelated children—a five-year-old girl, a two-year-old boy, and a five-month-old boy. While in Ethiopia, we met a nine-year-old girl who touched our hearts, and we returned to that country in 2008 to bring her home. Seven years later we unexpectedly became foster parents when

we were asked to provide a night's respite for a teen girl. She stayed for two and a half years and may have blessed us more than we blessed her.

While my role in this book has been to write primarily from my experience as a birth mother (also referred to as a first mother), I also share some of my life as an adoptive mom. I stand in the tension of being a former foster youth, a first mom, an adoptive mom, and a foster mom. The emotions are complicated, but I also have unique insight and great compassion for all members of the adoption triad. Jesus is writing a story with my life, and I will follow Him wherever He leads because my heart is completely in His hands.

Jodi's Story

Growing up in an adoptive family in the 1960s gave me a love and appreciation for adoption. My parents adopted two infants and always emphasized that my siblings had been specially chosen. (Although so much so that when I was a child, I was jealous of their not coming into the family in the boring way I had!)

As a young bride, I found myself in an infertile marriage. I pursued infertility treatments and domestic adoption at the same time and was thrilled to receive a newborn each way. Sadly, that marriage didn't survive, and I became a single mother parenting two precious little girls, one with straight blond hair and one with gorgeous biracial curls.

I lived my life as a single career woman until age forty-three. That's when God unexpectedly told me my future husband would come to the door of my house—and he did!

He arrived for our blind date sheepishly holding a bouquet of flowers behind his back, and I thought he was dreamy. We each had two children, his older than mine, and four seemed like plenty. We married, merged our families, and had no thought of more children. But as the saying goes, God had other plans.

Our church began serving the African Children's Choir, and before we knew what hit us, we'd traveled to East Africa and been wrecked with a love for orphans. We came home with a huge burden for the conditions of so many children trapped in orphanages around the world.

God was causing a revolution in our hearts, one we frankly needed. After years of climbing the ladder in corporate careers, we had dedicated our marriage to serving the Lord, and He took us seriously. Under the conviction of the Holy Spirit, we both pursued new jobs that allowed us to do ministry and give back. Next thing we knew, we had doubled the size of our family by adding four children from Uganda, aged seven, twelve, fourteen, and fifteen.

Along the way, we also stepped into other parenting roles with children in our path. We reached a point where we didn't

know how to answer when asked how many children we had. We'd look at each other, laugh, and say, "Well, it's complicated, but we have eight on our tax return."

It's clear that God intended to use our midlife marriage for us to devote the second half of our lives to His purposes. The last two decades have been an indescribable adventure of visiting vulnerable children on six continents and raising a family in which at least a half dozen birth parents are connected to us in some way. To say it's been messy and complicated would be a laughable understatement. God took our small idea of family and stretched ours into a more complex and colorful treasure than we could ever have imagined.

We wouldn't change a thing. As Isaiah 64:8 says, "You, LORD, are our Father. We are the clay, you are the potter; we are all the work of your hand."

You'll notice that throughout the book we've clearly identified which one of us is speaking. You may be tempted to read only from the person whose adoption position is the one to which you most relate, but we encourage you to read all our perspectives. When we listen to each other's stories, we gain greater understanding and compassion. And throughout this book, you can receive that greater understanding and compassion for the others in your adoption constellation. Additionally, each of us provides insights and information that applies outside of the position we represent, which will be helpful on your healing journey.

We believe in the good Father, who knew your story before you were even in it. He knew what would happen. And He's still writing your story. Most importantly, His desire is that you be healed, and that's why He led you to this book. Open your heart now to receive all God has for you.

PART ONE

ACKNOWLEDGING THE BROKENNESS

Why begin this book focusing on the hard aspects of adoption rather than the good? Why acknowledge the pain? The simple answer is we can't heal from wounds we don't name. Each adoptee and birth parent has experienced separation from the other. The circumstances may be vastly different, representing many different types of adoptions, but the separation remains.

Some adoptions are the result of court-ordered termination of parental rights. International adoptions may be completely closed with few details available, or open with communication between members of the first family and the adoptive family. Kinship adoptions are when one family member adopts the child of another. Carefully planned open adoptions—with openness ranging from annual letters and photos to regular visits—are increasingly common. In the past, many adoptions were closed, with mothers and babies separated and little information exchanged. There was little hope of reconnecting in the future.

With such a wide range of adoptions, it's difficult to speak with any kind of generality. Yet the primary experience that doesn't change is the separation of a child from the first parents—particularly the mother. To understand this loss we have to consider the prenatal experience.

Research shows that the mother and baby establish a relationship before the baby is even born. They're primed to know each other. The baby knows her mother's voice and can distinguish it from other women's voices from the time she's born.

> **The mother and baby establish a relationship before the baby is even born. They're primed to know each other.**

Neonatal research has found that newborns can recognize their mother on the basis of visual cues alone, by voice, and by odor.[1] Mothers also begin to know their babies before birth, becoming aware of when the baby is active, has hiccups, or seems to be peaceful and sleeping. One study found that during the third trimester, mothers began to see their infant as having the ability to interact with them:

> Some participants described their infants as actively participating in communication with them by moving toward abdominal stroking, extending a limb, or increasing/decreasing activity when certain voices were present.[2]

The mother is getting to know her child before the birth.

God designed mothers and babies to bond prenatally in preparation for building a secure attachment following the birth. When separation occurs following the birth, both the mother, whose body is physiologically prepared to nourish and care for her baby, and the baby, who has grown in her womb and knows her, experience a primal loss. This occurs regardless of the circumstances of the adoption.

A child who's adopted at an older age will experience a different depth of loss. If a mother has been unable to care for her child or the child has experienced neglect or abuse, healthy development is disrupted. The lesson of the first year of life is "I can trust."[3] Each time the baby expresses a need and the need is met, the baby learns their voice will be heard and

> The lesson of the first year of life is "I can trust."

their need met. The baby is hungry and cries, and a parent comes to feed them. The baby is cold or afraid, and the caregiver holds them close, warming and comforting them.

This happens thousands of times in the first year of life. Not only does this establish trust, but "the repeated completions of this cycle lay a strong foundation of self-worth, self-efficacy (the child knows he has a voice), self-regulation, and mental health."[4]

In their book *The Connected Parent*, Lisa C. Qualls and Dr. Karyn Purvis write:

> In optimal development, most children will grow up believing, "The world is a safe place. I'm going to be loved and cared for." But sadly, that is not the case with a child who has experienced relational trauma. Research tells us a child's ability to handle stress and to self-regulate as well as their later mental health can all be predicted by their early attachment relationships.[5]

Children in foster care commonly experience multiple placements resulting in a change of caregiver each time. A child whose mother is unable to care for them and is placed in an orphanage is also cared for by multiple caregivers. It's likely some are warm and nurturing and others are not. These changes are challenging for the developing child.

The good news is there is hope for healing. A child's early life may have been filled with relational complexity and loss, but the presence of safe, loving, adoptive parents has the potential to help that child heal. The love of God and the love of a trustworthy parent are transformative.

In one of his books, psychiatrist Dr. Bruce Perry writes, "The more healthy relationships a child has, the more likely he will be to recover from trauma and thrive. Relationships are the agents of change and the most powerful therapy is human love."[6] And in another book, Perry says the future can be bright in the presence of relational health:

> Our major finding is that your history of relational health—your connectedness to family, community, and culture—is more predictive of your mental health than your history of adversity. This is similar to the findings of other researchers looking at the power of positive relationships on health. Connectedness has the power to counterbalance adversity.[7]

In the following chapters we'll explore abandonment, grief and loss, shame and isolation, and trauma in the family. While these topics may feel weighty, we explore them with the sure knowledge that God can heal our hearts and minds. He can restore what has been lost or broken. We can find love and wholeness even when our circumstances have been far from perfect.

Hear in her own words how a young birth mother found healing and joy out of her brokenness.

BIRTH MOTHER—MARY CLOUD

Before, my life was driven by a hunger many young women know. At nineteen years old, I ached for a love I couldn't quite reach and feared I might not deserve. Still, I pursued it recklessly, feverishly, giving away bits of myself in exchange for even a taste of the love I craved. But the more I gave away, the less worthy I felt.

And then the appearance of two pink lines brought my reckless pursuit to a screaming halt. Suddenly, everything I did, everything I had done, mattered. And I was terrified.

Over the following months, the initial terror I felt at discovering I was pregnant settled into a general anxiety over the impossibilities of my future. Looking around at the mess I'd made, I recognized the gravity of my helpless state.

As I lay weeping on my bedroom floor, Jesus drew near, extending His hand. Desperate, I reached out and grabbed hold of the lifeline He offered us. "If you'll take us, you can have us," I told Him.

He took us both. And that decision led to another—adoption. My son was born, and he was perfect. Every inch of me cried as I left a part of myself behind at that hospital. But even as darkness threatened to consume me, God shone a light to guide me forward. Six months after giving birth, I received an email from my adoption worker. My son's adoptive parents wanted to know if I'd like to meet.

Though unsure, I agreed, eager to know it hadn't all been a dream, that he was real and that he was safe. That first meeting was admittedly awkward, but the joy I felt at seeing my son's face was worth it. He was going to be okay. We both were.

That was nine years ago, and I have not gone a year since without seeing my son. Today, I easily talk with his parents whether in person or over the phone. I get to play and talk with my boy as each year he grows to look more and more like my dad, like me. I get to tell him how much I love him and hear him say he loves me in return.

As for me, God has shown me a love greater and more valuable than any I ever dared to seek. He's never let me go but rather added to me even the love I once pursued. He's made me the wife of a wonderful husband. And He's made me a mother once again through the redemptive journey of foster care.

What unspeakable mercy, what bountiful blessings my God has poured out until my heart overflows. My light in the darkness, He has led me to a place I once thought impossible. And so I will follow Him all the way home.

TWO

ABANDONMENT

You created my inmost being; you knit me together in my mother's womb. — Psalm 139:13

ADOPTIVE MOM—JODI

It was a gorgeous April day, and the whole family was in the van heading home from an Easter Sunday service where our eldest adopted son had been baptized. When someone is baptized at our church, afterward a team of intercessors prays over the individual. My son, adopted at age fifteen, had not been raised by his parents, and with our other children present, the intercessors read Psalm 27:10: "Even if my father and mother abandon me, the LORD cares for me" (CSB).

Now we joyfully rode toward home, me thinking about what I needed to do to get Easter dinner on the table. Suddenly, my youngest son, also adopted, started hollering from the very back seat of the van. "Mom?"

I'm thinking about baked ham and ignoring him.

"Mom, Mom, Mom!" he yelled more emphatically over the chatter of his siblings.

Finally, I succumbed to his plea. "What is it, honey?"

"Was I abandoned?"

The van went silent. Everyone froze, including me. My husband was suddenly very interested in the workings of a traffic light, and I knew all the kids' eyes were on me, waiting to see how I'd handle the terrible pressure of this moment.

I didn't know what to do. I didn't know what to say. Yes, he had been abandoned as a toddler. But I was not at all prepared to face that story with him right then or any time on this busy holiday with guests imminently arriving. So I did the thing we as mothers must sometimes do. I punted.

"What do you think?" I asked.

I know, I know. Much better answers exist. But at that moment I had nothing to offer. His past was all too heavy and emotional to bring into that van full of Easter joy.

Looking back, though, I recognize that I should have been ready for that question. I should have prepared my own heart to have that conversation as each of my children was ready to have it. I should have had my talking points and my Scriptures ready. But I didn't. It took years for me to understand that the fear of abandonment, the wound of abandonment, was buried deep in the heart of each of my adopted children, whether that "abandonment" was done out of love by a birth parent at birth, out of brokenness and sin later, or by other circumstances that led to their being separated from their parents.

I also didn't understand just how long it would take, perhaps a lifetime, for this deep-seated fear of abandonment to stop rearing its ugly head.

One of my adopted daughters has a strong, determined personality. She excelled academically and had big career goals for herself, so college was always the plan for her future. But when the time came to choose which school, she didn't want to attend any of the excellent colleges in our state that would bring her a few hours from home. She wanted to stay home for college, and at the time, I felt that would have really limited her options.

So we pushed for her to choose a four-year university that was about two hours from our house.

Eventually, we got to the day when we joyfully moved her into her dorm room. The college years were hard on our relationship. She seemed more emotional and needy, and we had a difficult time finding our footing even during good times and college breaks. Everything just felt wobbly. While she seemed to be thriving at school, an undercurrent of unhappiness was directed toward us as her parents.

Finally, during the drive to college at the beginning of her senior year, she confessed to me that she absolutely hated being taken back to school each semester because she always believed we wouldn't come back for her.

I was speechless. How could she possibly believe that for even an instant? How could she even consider this possibility when we had consistently poured out our love and commitment to her for many years since her adoption?

But there it was. That fear of abandonment was seated so deeply in her soul that it colored her worldview and her reality. There was no evidence that we would leave her, but powerful memories and wounds were just below the surface, making her feel insecurely attached to us and our family.

Learning of her worry was heartbreaking to me. I'm so fortunate that I was born into a loud and loving family and have never experienced being abandoned. The hardest thing for me to face as an adoptive mother is that someone—especially a mother—could abandon my child. The bond between mother and child feels like the most powerful bond on earth. Once so connected that their very bodies were interdependent, how can this connection ever be broken? My heart struggles to comprehend how a mother could make this choice, and I'm filled with anger and judgment.

And then I remember the Word of God—where God points me back to His story, the story of His people, and I see that right there at the very beginning of the Bible, God left for us a story about abandonment. Jochebed, Moses' birth mother, lived a life of misery and suffering as a woman enslaved by the Egyptian empire. Survival was her only goal. When she finds herself pregnant and a death edict has been issued over all newborn babies, she abandons her son Moses by placing him in a basket to float on the Nile River.

She did this not out of neglect but out of love. She did this out of her desperation. This was her only hope—to believe there was a tiny chance that he could live and thrive if she let him go. And so she made the most agonizing of choices, a choice that would leave her marked forever. She abandoned her child to save him. Moses is found and adopted by Pharaoh's daughter, giving us one of the most compelling stories of redemptive adoption in the Bible (Exodus 2).

And suddenly it all looks different, doesn't it? I've never had to face the torment of living a life of such desperation, but so many women even today live in circumstances of poverty and survival. Suddenly, my judgment is washed away. I turn the spotlight on myself, on my own critical heart and my own self-righteousness. Could my child's abandonment have been an act of deeper love?

We are reminded of all the birth parents who believe their treasured infant would be better loved by someone more equipped. We are reminded of the women and even fathers who surrender their children to orphanages just so their son or daughter won't go hungry. We are reminded of the families who have lost their children to the foster care system and are desperately trying to get them back. Suddenly, abandonment comes through a different lens. Suddenly, it turns on its side and can be framed as an act of the most sacrificial form of love.

Now I can open the door to understanding and forgiveness. While not all abandonment of children may be done out of a higher love, the understanding that it's a possibility creates a perspective that softens my heart. And more importantly, it frames this experience another way for my child. God was still there when Moses was abandoned.

How can I give this perspective to my adopted children? How can I share this holy perspective from the very Word of God? How can I help them embrace this sacred truth that God was still there so their own story of abandonment can become a story of the deepest love over their life? How can they know that the very thing they may believe was a ruinous injury is not the end of their story?

> How can I help my children embrace the sacred truth that God was still there so their own story of abandonment can become a story of the deepest love over their life?

This perspective reframes my daughter's story and reconstructs the narrative. Not only for her soul to heal but also for my own judgmental heart to be set free from anger toward her birth parent. This is the power of knowing the Word of God. This is why we must read Scripture and study its truths.

Freedom Prayer for Adoptive Parents

Please read this entire freedom-giving prayer before praying it. Then pray the parts relevant for you, adding anything you think needs to be included and remembering to engage your heart. Also, of course, use the pronoun that fits your child.

Last, the spiritual prayer elements of repentance, forgiveness, and release are clearly labeled in this Freedom Prayer and those through chapter 5. After that, we believe you'll have become so familiar with these areas that you'll recognize and appreciate the progression in each prayer without the labels.

Lord, thank you that you are a God who will never leave me nor my child, that you will certainly never forsake us. Today I ask you to empower me as I deal with this issue of abandonment.

Repent

Please forgive me for the following (select what's applicable to you):

- *not really dealing with my own abandonment issues so I'm more easily triggered by my child's problems*
- *anger and judgment against my child's birth mother for her abandonment and the resulting deep hurt and fear*
- *any way I've wrongly spoken to my child about their birth mother*
- *my slowness to recognize times when my child's challenging behavior was coming out of their abandonment and fear of abandonment*
- *taking on the burden of trying to make up for my child's past wounds when you, Lord, are the only one who can heal their wounds*
- *not establishing my child in the truth that you are their true parent who is always there for them*
- *(your additions)*

Lord, I choose to receive your forgiveness. (Pause and receive God's forgiveness.) *And based on your forgiveness, I choose to forgive myself.* (Now forgive yourself.)

Forgive Others

Now forgive everyone who contributed to your abandonment as well as to your child's abandonment.

Lord, I choose to forgive
- *all those who have abandoned me in any way*
- *my child's birth parent for choosing to abandon them even if it was for their good*
- *those who have judged me or my family as we've failed to always know how to help our child*
- *my child's birth mother (and/or father) for being critical of me and how I'm raising my child*
- *my child's birth parents for competing with me/us for my/our child's love*
- *my child for abandoning me*
- *for all the ways I've felt abandoned by my adoption agency for not preparing me properly or giving me enough information*
- *(your additions)*

Lord, help me continue to express forgiveness to others as difficult situations arise.

Release

If you're a visual person, we encourage you to "see" yourself giving the abandonment to the Lord or laying it at the foot of His cross.

Lord, I'm ready to release to you the abandonment and all the pain I've experienced because of my child's abandonment. I release the following:
- *my own pain of abandonment (pre-adoption)*
- *the pain of at times feeling abandoned by my child*
- *disappointment and frustration with my child's abandonment issues and fears and their resulting negative behavior cycles*

- *the fear of ultimately being abandoned by my child*
- *my sense of failure in trying to help my child with their abandonment wounds*
- *feelings of inadequacy and sometimes failure when trying to share with my child your great love for them*
- *(any additional issues you've experienced)*

Thank you, Lord, for taking my pain around abandonment issues. Help me feel so loved by you that love can overflow from my heart to my child's heart. Please grow my faith so strong that I become completely confident that you will never leave me or forsake me. Empower me to bring the truth of your love and your constant presence to my child in such a way that they can understand it and believe it.

Lord, please establish in my child the reality of your loving presence. Let that reality color their emotions and be the lens through which they see themselves and the world. Heal my child's abandonment and rejection wounds and take away their fears.

In Jesus' name I pray, amen.

BIRTH MOTHER—LISA

I knew I was pregnant when I started vomiting in the bathroom each morning during Honors English. The school year was winding down, and I had kept my secret tucked away. Only my boyfriend and my best friend knew. When my parents found out, they were angry and terrified—what were they going to do? One thing was clear: they needed to get me as far away from my boyfriend as possible.

They turned to the church for advice. The era of maternity homes for unwed mothers was coming to a close as teen girls began keeping their babies. The alternative solution was to place me in foster care through an agency. One day a social worker picked me up in her white VW Bug and drove me north to a large city. We stopped in front of an olive-green house on a busy city street where the door was answered by a young mom in her early thirties. She was recently divorced and had two young daughters. She also ran a day care in her home. I loved children, so helping in the day care came naturally to me.

She originally had me share a bedroom with her young daughter. I felt totally out of place and uncomfortable. I was used to having my own room, and everything in this house felt chaotic. At the end of the hall was a large closet used for storage. I asked if I could make that my bedroom. It was just big enough to fit a twin bed even if I couldn't open the door all the way. I loved having my own tiny space.

I was cut off from every person I knew and loved. Long-distance phone calls were expensive, and I had no means of paying for them. Thankfully, I found a job babysitting for a woman who worked for the phone company and had free long distance. I babysat in exchange for the opportunity to call my boyfriend and other friends at home. I was desperate to hear the voices of people I loved and who knew me.

I attended a large high school, much larger than my school at home. When I learned there were honors classes, I went to the office and asked to have my schedule changed. I was a good student, but that's not how they saw me. I was a pregnant foster kid. Clearly, they believed I wasn't a good or smart kid. But thankfully they did change my schedule, allowing me to be in classes that challenged me.

It was the loneliest year of my life—almost a form of torture to be isolated and unknown. I felt rejected and abandoned. As an adult all these years later, I know my parents were doing their best to cope with a situation they never imagined they would be in. Sending me away seemed like the right thing to do at the time. But it was also a powerful tool the adoption agency used to exert influence over me and induce fear.

One night while babysitting, I talked with my boyfriend. We had plans. After our baby was born, I would move back to our town and live with him in his mom's house. She would help us with our baby until we could make it on our own. My boyfriend would turn eighteen the month after our baby was born and would graduate in June. We could make it work.

But that night he broke up with me and told me not to call him when our baby was born. My baby and I were alone in the world. I curled up on the sofa with my arms wrapped around my belly and sobbed. The pressure to give up my baby had been heavy, and I had fought as hard as I could. But in that moment, abandoned by everyone, I wondered if I had lost the battle.

I told my social worker I was considering adoption and had called a couple of agencies. She looked at me in surprise and explained that my foster agency was also my adoption agency. I was in foster care with the plan that I would give them my baby and he would be placed with a couple in their program. Until that moment, I hadn't understood the system, and I was quickly put in my place. The plan from the very beginning was not to care for me and help me care for my baby; it was to house me until I paid my debt to God and society and gave them my child.

Initially, my foster mom had supported my efforts to prepare for my baby. She took me to yard sales to buy baby clothes and taught me how to sew flannel diapers. But then the agency told her if I kept my baby, she couldn't help me in any way. I couldn't continue living with her. When she told me this years later, she felt terrible. But at the time she'd been afraid to go against the church and even worried she might be breaking the law if she helped me. She feared she might even lose custody of her own children.

I didn't want to give them my child. But I also had no one in the world to help me keep him. My baby and I had been abandoned—or so I believed. I didn't know it yet, but the Lord had never left me.

Freedom Prayer for Birth Moms

Please read this entire freedom-giving prayer before praying it. Then pray the parts relevant for you, adding anything you think needs to be included and remembering to engage your heart. Also, of course, use the pronoun that fits your child.

Last, the spiritual prayer elements of repentance, forgiveness, and release are clearly labeled in this Freedom Prayer and in those through chapter 5. After that, we believe you'll have become so familiar with these areas that you'll recognize and appreciate the progression in each prayer without the labels.

> *Lord, I thank you that you are a God of new beginnings, and today is a new beginning for me. I ask you to empower me as I deal with this issue of abandonment.*

Repent
Please forgive me for the following (select what's applicable to you):
- *having sex outside of marriage*
- *judging all those who didn't support me at a time I needed support the most (name them one by one)*
- *ALL judgments and bitterness toward my social worker and adoption agency*
- *competing with my child's adoptive parents for my child's love.*

- *holding on to criticalness, self-hate, or unforgiveness toward my child's adoptive parents*
- *every way I felt you abandoned me when my prayers weren't answered*
- *(add anything else that fits for you)*

Lord, I choose to receive your forgiveness. (Pause and receive God's forgiveness.) *And based on your forgiveness, I choose to forgive myself.* (Now forgive yourself.)

Forgive Others

Now forgive everyone who contributed to your being/feeling abandoned.

Lord, I choose to forgive
- *all those I thought would support me but did not (name them specifically)*
- *harsh judgments others made toward me because I was pregnant or gave up my child*
- *social workers and/or the adoption agency for not being clear about their plans or expectations for my baby*
- *any deception or manipulation involved in the adoption process*
- *anyone who made me feel forced to give up my child*
- *those who in the process of adoption stole my self-respect, value, and confidence*
- *the adoptive parents who have made things more difficult and stressful than necessary*
- *(your additions)*

Lord, thank you that you promise your presence will always be with me and my child.

Release

If you're a visual person, we encourage you to "see" yourself giving the abandonment and fear of abandonment to the Lord or laying them at the foot of His cross.

Lord, I'm ready to release to you the abandonment and all negative associated feelings I've carried. I release the following:

- *all fear of further abandonment and rejection*
- *any guilt around abandoning my child*
- *past trauma and the desperation, isolation, and loneliness that went with it*
- *all victimization and all bitterness*
- *the pain around saying goodbye to my child and the intense pain I feel on their birthday or holidays*
- *all frustration, anger, or resentment toward the adoption system*
- *all fear that my child's adoptive family has said negative things to my child to turn them against me*
- *every way the adoptive family has made connecting with my child difficult*
- *(your additions)*

Thank you, Lord, for taking my pain. Please continue to heal my broken heart, as well as my child's heart, of all abandonment wounds. Enable us both to live full and healthy lives. Help me see your hand in past events as well as in my future. In Jesus' name, amen.

ADOPTEE—BETSY

It was a normal Saturday morning. Jenny, Gail, and I—all six-year-olds—were sitting on the floor playing with dolls. I was stuffing my doll's head through the neck opening in the pink dress my grandmother had made for her. Playing happily, I was completely unprepared for what was about to happen.

Jenny spoke up. "You know, your parents aren't your real parents. You don't have any real parents."

I was shocked. What was she saying? That couldn't be true! But her words somehow connected with something deep in the pit of my stomach. A monster who'd been lying there quietly suddenly sprang to life. My abandonment wound had been ripped open. I instantly felt chilled to the core. My belly churned, there was a lump in my throat, and all at once questions leaped up for the first time. They came flying at me like a flock of angry birds, relentlessly attacking my mind.

These were new questions I'd never asked before. *Who are my real parents? Why didn't they want me? Who am I? Do I really belong to anyone?*

"Stop. Shut up," I said, protesting with all the strength I could muster on such short notice. "I don't want to listen to you."

I didn't know this monster's name was Abandonment. Looking back, I'm glad I didn't know I would be at war with this monster for thirty-one years. Not until God's healing truth poured oil into the wounds of my torn and raw heart was Abandonment dealt a death blow.

Holding back tears, I fought with the best defense I had—my incredible adoption story. After all, I knew every line of it by heart.

I knew how the adoption agency had let my parents know they had a special little girl for them. How my mother had interrupted my father's classes at the college where he taught to tell him the exciting news. How they had driven ever so fast to the Children's Home Society in Greensboro to meet me. How they walked into the room where I was, and even though they saw several other babies as well, they knew I was theirs.

"Here is our little girl. This is the daughter God has given us" was their joyful response.

This was the truth I wanted to believe. I did have real parents! I did belong. Bravely, I shared this story.

Up to this moment, this story had defined me. It had given me a secure identity. I was specially chosen, just right for my adoptive parents. But suddenly, the foundation of the identity I thought I had was shattered. It felt as if the anchor establishing my life had been dislodged.

When the voice of a deep wound contends against the voice of logic and knowledge, do you know which one usually wins? That's right. The voice of the wound always shouts louder and more emphatically. Logic loses, and as it slinks away, hurt takes over.

This battle for my sense of belonging and for my identity would rage for years through many heated skirmishes. To deal with abandonment and the fear of abandonment that travels with it, I came to what seemed like an obvious conclusion: I couldn't risk upsetting my parents, causing them to consider giving me back to the adoption agency. I had to please them at all costs. I had to hide my negative emotions and not risk sharing my inner conflicts. My mantra was *Don't tell anyone. I must make them believe I'm "fine."*

And so began my secret life. Ever so deceptively, I began to lie to my parents. I lied about my real feelings because I was determined to look fine in their eyes. Looking back, it's amazing how easy it was. I seemed to have a talent for lying.

Another part of my secret life was covering up the paralyzing fear of death that tormented me nightly. As evening approached, dread fell over me like a heavy dark cloak. *What if tonight is the night I'll die?* The faintest noise paralyzed me. I was on high alert. I often fought sleepiness until my parents went to bed so I could turn on my light. At least I would see my killer and not be surprised. This torturous fear of death lasted well into adulthood. How would I be able to tell my future husband I needed to sleep with a light on?

Nor did I ever mention the sexual fantasies I had of people being naked or the curious stimulation I felt from the fantasies. *How could I be so nasty?* I asked myself, never finding an answer. And what if my parents knew?

Abandonment is the root of all negative roots in the orphan's heart, and it certainly was in my own heart. It connects to almost every negative emotion or lack. It could be thought of as a unique highway system where roads all have the same starting place. It could also be compared to a corporation with many divisions. These could be called fear of abandonment, attachment challenges,[1] rejection, self-rejection, self-hate, expected rejection, neglect, trauma, fear, not belonging, anger and rebellion, hiding, and isolation. When triggered, abandonment can move at a raging pace, take over, and demand center stage. It's relentless.

Abandonment is the root of all negative roots in the orphan's heart.

One of the deadliest things about abandonment is the expectations it produces. Consider for a moment the phases of the Belief-Expectation Cycle.[2] Here's a simple explanation of that cycle:

1. The lies we believe (our ungodly beliefs) are formed out of a hurtful experience (i.e., abandonment).
2. Our expectations about our own lives come out of these lies ("I expect to be abandoned 'again'").
3. I behave in such a way that I influence how others treat me. My ungodly expectations draw to me people who will abandon me.
4. Every time I experience abandonment "again," it just confirms that the lie I'm believing is "true." ("See, I told you so. I knew I would be abandoned 'again.'")

As Job put it, "The thing I greatly feared has come upon me" (Job 3:25 NKJV).

Another destructive feature of abandonment is that it drives an invisible wedge between the adoptee or foster child and the parents. It creates a space that's hard for each one to navigate. Although it's not a place to point fingers, we do need to recognize that abandonment is there. It insists on being reckoned with.

Even though I grew up in a Christian home, abandonment undermined my ability to believe God's Word. I could only partly believe that He would never leave me nor forsake me.[3] How could I believe God's Word that said He "chose us in Him before the foundation of the world" (Ephesians 1:4 NKJV)? Most often it felt like these great Scriptures were for other people, not for me. The abandonment monster within me continued to scream, "No, no, no. Not for you!"

Yes, it significantly helped that my parents consistently heaped their love upon me. And yet it was still a tough go. Not until God touched my abandonment wound did healing come—healing that allowed me to receive His truth for myself.

Freedom Prayer for Adoptees

Please read this entire freedom-giving prayer before praying it. Then pray the parts relevant for you, adding anything you think needs to be included and remembering to engage your heart.

Last, the spiritual prayer elements of repentance, forgiveness, and release are clearly labeled in this Freedom Prayer and in those through chapter 5. After that, we believe you'll have become so familiar with these areas that you'll recognize and appreciate the progression in each prayer without the labels.

Lord, I thank you that you are a God of new beginnings, and today is a new beginning for me. I ask you to empower me as I deal with abandonment.

Repent

Please forgive me for the following (select what's applicable to you):

- ways I've blamed my birth mother for giving me up
- ways I've acted out because of my abandonment pain
- hiding, withdrawing, and becoming "invisible"
- believing the lie that I'm worthless
- acting out in rage, anger, or retaliation
- intentionally hurting others
- lying
- all self-destructive acts (for example, cutting, suicide attempts, or filling yourself with unhealthy substances or influences such as drugs, destructive music, or porn)
- living out of rejection, self-rejection, or expected rejection
- (your additions)

Lord, I choose to receive your forgiveness. (Pause and receive God's forgiveness.) *And based on your forgiveness, I choose to forgive myself.* (Now forgive yourself.)

Forgive Others

Now forgive everyone who contributed to your abandonment.

Lord, I choose to forgive

- my birth mom/parents for abandoning me and all the pain of rejection and insecurity that resulted
- my birth mom/parents for my identity struggles and confusion about who I am

- my birth mother/father for their part of my forming unhealthy patterns as I tried to deal with my pain
- my adoptive parent(s) for not knowing how to deal with me at times
- (for open adoption) my birth parents for the stress and confusion that having both an adoptive family and a birth family has brought to my life
- (your additions)

Lord, thank you for leading me in forgiveness. I commit to forgiving others as you show me additional forgiveness that's needed. I've lived out of abandonment and the fear of more abandonment way too long. Today I want to begin to remove it. I ask you to help me move forward and totally conquer this area that has so limited my life.

Release

If you're a visual person, we encourage you to "see" yourself giving the abandonment to the Lord or laying it at the foot of His cross.)

Lord, I'm ready to release to you the abandonment, the fear of abandonment, and the rejection that have had such a powerful influence in my life. I release the following:

- *anger, blame, or criticalness I've held toward my birth parents*
- *fear of further abandonment*
- *pain of not knowing who I am*
- *pain of feeling like an "outsider," like I don't belong*
- *pain and confusion of having two families*
- *pain of harmful or self-destructive behaviors*
- (add anything else you want to release)

Lord, thank you for taking my abandonment, rejection, and fears. Please plant your truth about my identity into my heart. Please establish in me the truth that no matter how the egg and sperm came together, it was you who created me, you who watched over me as I was being formed in my mother's womb, and you who had a plan and a purpose for my life.[4]

Thank you for always having a special place in your heart for anyone who's been orphaned—and that includes me. I receive you as my primary Father, the One who will never leave me nor forsake me. Please continue to heal my heart and establish within me your truth.

In Jesus' name, amen.

THREE

GRIEF AND LOSS

The LORD is close to the brokenhearted and saves those who are crushed in spirit. —Psalm 34:18

ADOPTIVE MOM—JODI

I opened my social media and was surprised to find a message from a relative of our adopted children. She let me know their grandfather was suffering from an illness and asked us to pray for him. Of course we eagerly agreed.

As my teen daughter came down the stairs to get breakfast, I delivered the news to her. I knew she loved this grandfather and would want to be updated. But I was completely unprepared for what came next. Grief came over her like a tsunami. Although her grandfather wasn't gravely ill and would recover, this news jolted her and unleashed her buried grief over the loss of her father as a small child. In a matter of moments, she was doubled over, wracked with tears, rocking wildly on the couch. I could do nothing but hold her tiny body as she heaved, and I prayed for her.

Until that moment I hadn't known my child carried the weight of all that grief just below the surface. Yes, I knew my children had experienced many losses, including the loss of being raised by their birth parents. But I didn't understand that the trauma of her father's sudden death was a huge burden of weight my daughter carried every day. No one had talked to her about this loss. No one had helped her process it as a child. Talking about feelings wasn't common in her culture, and she had no outlet for her grief. The boulder of it traveled with her.

And this is why, on a Tuesday morning, she could hear of her grandfather being temporarily ill and be completely overtaken with grief without warning. When I saw this, I knew I needed to give her the space to talk about her father and that loss.

The life of an adoptive mother is a life of reframing loss and grief for both for me and my child, but I had no idea about that when I entered this journey. In adoption and foster care, the dream of how a family will be built needs to change. Facing the loss of that dream will allow grief to be part of our relationship as we heal together as parent and child.

This new dream must be built on past tragedy. I see now how wrong I was to think of adoption as just a beautiful thing—it's also sometimes tragic for the birth family. A second family is always "plan B." It's not God's design for a child to move from one family to another. His design is two thriving, biological parents with children protected, loved, and nurtured until adulthood. But brokenness, sin, and death have entered that perfect design for an adoption to be needed. And so the shadow of grief and loss can hover over an adoptive family like a storm cloud.

In my experience, during the training for foster care and adoption, little was said about grief. Rightly, great emphasis is placed on the joy of receiving a child into one's home. But as soon as the child arrives, the grief they carry with them steps through the door as well. Many foster children live in the unspeakable tension of wondering if they will be permanently separated from their parents. Adopted children have already experienced loss in profound ways, perhaps more deeply than we as their second parents can even understand. We can't hope for healing and cohesion as a family unless we face grief and loss. A child has experienced a loss, and all that loss enters our family.

Looking back, I understand this so much more profoundly. The clues were there, but I didn't comprehend them. I wondered why my son grew solemn as his birthday approached. Why did questions about parties and cake colors and friends coming turn my little boy toward gloomy reflection? I didn't know family occasions meant to be happy—like birthdays and holidays— would be overshadowed with the grief and loss my children had already experienced. I didn't know they would be reminders of the lost first family.

I have been told that some infant adoptees find great sorrow in the day they were born because they were separated from their birth mother on that day. I remember meeting my adopted infant like it was yesterday. The day of my daughter's birth was one of the most joyous days of my life. I walked into a dark infant intensive care hospital room and saw an angelic form of the tiniest baby lying amid blinking lights and tubes. And I thought she was the most beautiful creature I'd ever seen. I felt I had received a gift beyond any measure. I couldn't even comprehend the immensity of someone giving me such a gift.

While I was filled with great joy on that day, I can see now that birthdays and other family holidays like Mother's Day are very complicated for my children. I can't fix this for them. No matter how many cakes I bake or balloons I buy, I can't fix these losses.

Whether living or deceased, biological relatives are like ghosts in the adoptive family constellation, and they must be grieved. When I see a beautiful Christmas card photo of our diverse adoptive family wearing matching sweaters, my child may see the people missing from the photo—those who have been lost.

Grief hovers, and a foster or adoptive parent can never know when it might be triggered by a sound, a smell, or food that reminds the child of a memory with their birth family. For a foster child, a blue sweater on display in a mall might be the exact shade their birth father was wearing the last time they saw him. Moments later, the child is having a meltdown in the middle of JCPenney, and the foster mother has absolutely no idea why.

This is the unpredictable, messy, triggering constellation we enter when we make the choice to love a child who was born to another. We make a choice to live in their loss.

But it's not just the child's grief we have to face in this life. It may also be our own. Many couples face infertility as a path to the choice to adopt. Infertility itself is a huge loss. It's a loss of the dream of biological children, of the perfect family, of what is seen as normal. When a couple faces infertility, they have to accept that their journey will not be simple or conventional. The path to children will be complicated. Other people will have to be involved in the most intimate of experiences. The sorrow of infertility can be particularly disturbing for a woman, as much of a woman's identity and self-worth can be attached to her journey as a mother.

Yes, many of us say we always wanted to adopt or that God called us to adopt. And those things can definitely be true. But if we're honest, many of us have to confess we're in this place because another kind of loss took place. In my case, infertility was the reason I first adopted. And infertility was a crushing loss—the loss of my dream of "my children" followed later by the loss of my marriage. I had to face divorce and the end of my hope for a picture-perfect life, a conventional life, a "whole" family (or so I thought!).

Many adopted children must live with the reality that, because of infertility, they are their adoptive parents' second choice. Deep down this must be felt, even on an unconscious level.

And even for those who choose to adopt for religious or charitable reasons, as I later did, an adoptive family represents the loss of a perfect family in the eyes of the world. While to me my family now seems exceptionally beautiful, to others it may seem less than ideal, a patchwork, a secondhand version, a messy version.

As an adoptive parent, I have lost the dream of my family being formed in a certain way—biologically. And my child is living in an ongoing state of loss, having lost his or her first family even if that family is or was less than ideal. It's easy for me to gloss over this and tell myself my child must be happy to be in a "good" or "loving" family. But some adopted children wish their biological family would have had the capacity to raise them. So no matter how loving or wonderful we are, we must accept that we may be our adopted child's second choice—plan B.

> No matter how loving or wonderful we are, we must accept that we may be our adopted child's second choice—plan B.

This, then, is how the relationship begins. Both parties, deep down, can end up with their second choice, their plan B, their consolation prize for a family.

How do you build a family, a solid rock, an unending and enduring bond on this dynamic? How do you make a beautiful family when it's based on so much grief and loss?

In our humanity, we can't. It's impossible and unlikely and against our very nature. We'll always know we're dealing with plan B. There's only one way this can become whole, only one way it makes sense—redemption. Without the idea of redemption, loss is just loss. It's an aching hole that never goes away. But if we understand and embrace the stunningly gorgeous beauty of redemption through the love of God, everything is possible. Anything is possible.

Grief may be part of the story, but there's also a chance for great hope and joy. I have experienced this pure joy and seen it in our family.

Prayer is the key to this understanding. When I pray as I'm grieving, I open the door for God to heal my heart. I welcome Him into the tender places that ache in my soul. I believe that He can redeem the loss through His supernatural power. And with that power through prayer, when my daughter grieves, I can grieve with her. I can sit with her in her grief and not try to brush it away or dismiss it. I can have the courage to admit that, yes, there is grief, but there can also be healing and hope. Because I know the source of that healing and hope and how to access it.

This book is all about the journey toward that healing and hope. We live in an imperfect world where we face grief and loss daily. But God is walking with us before it, through it, and making a way for us to find wholeness after it.

Keep reading, beloved.

Freedom Prayer for Adoptive Parents

Please read this entire freedom-giving prayer before praying it. Then pray the parts relevant for you, adding anything you think needs to be included and remembering to engage your heart. Also, of course, use the pronoun that fits your child.

> *Lord, please help me as I look at this whole area of grief and loss. I want to clean out any old debris that's cluttering my heart or soul.*

Repent

Please forgive me for the following (select what's applicable to you):

- *not processing my own loss and grief as I gave up my vision for "the perfect family"*
- *inadequacy/failure in helping my child process their losses and grief*
- *not understanding the extent of my child's loss/trauma*
- *not recognizing that adoption has a tragic part as well as a joyful part (often tragic for both the birth mom and child)*
- *any resentment toward social workers or the adoption agency for not better preparing me for the ways my child's loss and grief can affect their life*
- *my sense of loss when my child didn't bond with me or return my love*
- *not turning to you, Lord, for help*
- *(your additions)*

Lord, I choose to receive your forgiveness. (Pause and receive God's forgiveness.) *And based on your forgiveness, I choose to forgive myself.* (Now forgive yourself.)

Forgive Others

Now forgive everyone who contributed to your own losses as well as to your child's losses and grief.

Lord, I choose to forgive

- *anyone, including myself, related to the losses that led me to consider adoption*
- *people who caused my child to experience the loss of their first family*

- myself, for my own failure to deal with my losses and grief as well as my child's losses and grief
- (your additions)

Lord, thank you for your peace that forgiving others brings into my life. I receive that peace now.

Release

Lord, I'm ready to release to you the pain I've carried around because of my own losses and grief as well as my child's. I release the following:

- the pain and loss in my life that led me to adopt a child
- any grief and loss about not having more of my own biological children
- the pain and loss of not being first in my child's heart
- the pain of not feeling accepted or appreciated by my child
- grief around occasions when my child's loss was triggered and a beautiful event was sabotaged
- all the what-ifs that torment me. For example, what if I had better understood that my child's behavior pointed to their loss and grief?
- all the sense of failure and pain of my child expressing hate for me or attacking me because of their pain
- (add anything else relevant to you)

Lord, please replace these terrible losses and this grief with your deep comfort, the comfort only you can provide. Thank you for healing my heart. In Jesus' name, amen.

BIRTH MOTHER—LISA

Nothing could have prepared me for the devastating grief I experienced when I lost my son to adoption. We had spent nine months together, him curled safely in my womb, me with my arms around both of us keeping us as safe as I could.

He was born on a cold winter night. I struggled through labor, which was far more difficult than I ever imagined. Despite my foster mom dozing by my side, I felt profoundly alone in my suffering. I had taken childbirth preparation classes and learned how to breathe in complex patterns, but as the intensity of the contractions increased, I was reduced to simply breathing in and out and trying to keep from losing control. I was afraid of being sedated and missing even a moment of my baby's life.

In pain and fear, I felt more alone than I had in my entire life. The contractions continued, one after another, and my desperation grew. But I'd been learning about Jesus and sensing His presence more and more. Knowing I couldn't make it through this on my own, I cried out to God, and He met me in a powerful way. Jesus was with me in the delivery room that day. He carried me through my son's birth while also birthing a lifelong journey of faith in me. The day my son was born is the day I was born anew in Christ.

My son was born and laid on my chest, and I cried tears of joy and sheer relief. For three days I kept him with me in the hospital, only returning him to the nursery when the nurses insisted. I named him Christopher, and I prayed over him in the simplest ways. I also cried many tears.

I had never loved anyone so fiercely in my life. How could anyone think I would survive losing my son? How could it possibly be good to entrust him to the care of strangers, even strangers who'd been carefully vetted? I didn't even know their names, yet I was expected to give them my cherished and loved child and never see him again.

A friend recently told me about attending a funeral for a baby who'd been stillborn. The parents wept loudly, expressing sorrow that reached deep into their souls. They loved this baby even though they had never seen her take a breath or looked into her eyes. The bond of love was created while this little one grew in her mother's womb. They prayed for her, talked to her, dreamed of a future with her and all the special things to come—her first words, her first steps, her learning to read, her graduating from high school, her falling in love.

A birth mother is expected to say goodbye to her child and move on with life as if her heart hasn't just been ripped from her chest.

Her life was already precious and held with so much hope, but it was all wrenched away in a moment when the ultrasound showed a little heart no longer beating. Their grief was real, and raw, and understood. Their family cried with them, and their church surrounded them offering comfort with meals, cards, and flowers. These parents were on a journey that was theirs alone. Nobody could make it move more quickly, but they were held in the hearts of everyone who loved them.

In contrast, a birth mother is expected to say goodbye to her child and move on with life as if her heart hasn't just been ripped from her chest. God designed us mothers to form attachment with our babies. We're hormonally prepared to care for our newborns. Our bodies make milk to nourish them, our hearing is heightened to hear their cries, and our bodies literally long for them.

This was decades ago, and still I remember the overwhelming love I felt for my son during those three days. Wrapped in the blanket I'd clumsily made, Christopher rested on my chest tucked under my chin. Tears fell on his sweet head as I prayed for him.

I knew I wouldn't be able to bear leaving him in the hospital and walking away when the day came to say goodbye. So I made a plan to take him from the hospital to the agency. My foster mother and I were supposed to drive straight there, but we were both so stricken with grief that she pulled into a parking lot overlooking Puget Sound to give us extra time. We held Christopher, cried, and prayed.

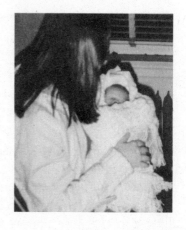

At the office, the agency director and my foster mom left me alone to say a final goodbye. Then when my foster mom said it was time, I rose from the chair, kissed my son's forehead one more time, and placed him in the arms of the agency director. Everything in me wanted to snatch him back or get down on my knees and plead for help, but I turned and walked out the door. Three steps down the hallway, I collapsed.

I didn't know how I could walk away. But I believed what I'd been told—that I had nothing to offer my son and no place to go. Nobody was going to help me, and we would be homeless. I stood, held my foster mom's arm, and walked out of the building.

This was the era when some progressive agencies were beginning to offer semi-open adoptions, but most adoptions were still closed. My social worker gave me some basic information about my son's new parents but no promise of letters or photos. They were a wonderful, educated, financially stable couple who hadn't been able to have a child biologically and could give my son everything he would ever need.

I didn't know then that severing the bond between us would be a wound he would also carry forever. Years later, after we reconnected, he told me that despite my love, prayers, and longing for him to have a better life than I could provide, there was no escaping the sense that he'd been abandoned. The one person who should have loved him and fought for him had walked away. Intellectually, he understood that I had tried so hard to keep him, but deep in his heart he felt the loss.

When parents announce they have adopted, people recognize that a longing of their hearts has been fulfilled. But the birth mother's grief journey is just beginning. I've rarely met a birth mom who hasn't continued grieving. This is due in part to disenfranchised grief. Disenfranchised grief is a grief not acknowledged by society.[1] My son was born when many young women kept their babies, but many others chose abortion or were sent away to give birth and then return as though nothing had happened. There was so much shame surrounding being an unwed mother that many families kept these secrets to their graves.

After losing my son, I returned to my foster home. And as Christmas break ended a week later, I walked back through the doors of my high school as if nothing had changed. I sat in geometry class pretending I was the same person I'd been just weeks before. But nothing was the same—my body and mind were yearning for my newborn. I wondered if I would begin screaming, sobbing, and be removed from school. Would they put me in a hospital for people who had lost their grip on reality?

Decades later, my family suffered a terrible car accident, and our thirteen-year-old daughter did not survive. We were in shock, overwhelmed, and devastated. As the news spread, family and friends began arriving at our home. Flowers and cards arrived daily. On the day of her memorial service, I was filled with fear. Could I make it through the service? Would I begin sobbing and be unable to stop?

When we entered the church, the room was thick with love. I sensed God's presence in a powerful way. Hundreds of people sang with us, cried with us, and prayed with us. They waited in a long line to hug us and offer kind words. We were not alone in our sorrow. Months later, at church or in the grocery store, people continued to hug me and ask how I was doing. They expressed their sorrow at our loss.

The contrast between the experience of losing my son and losing my daughter was extreme. One was hidden and forgotten, disenfranchised grief. The other was public and acknowledged.

Another aspect of the loss a birth parent experiences is ambiguous loss.[2] Ambiguous loss, a term coined by Pauline Boss, occurs when it's highly unlikely a person will reach emotional closure or have a clear understanding of the situation. One type of ambiguous loss occurs when a loved one is physically absent but still very much alive to the person experiencing the loss. In extreme cases this may involve a family member missing in military action or a child who was taken by an estranged partner and simply disappeared. This is what losing my son felt like—he was lost somewhere in the world, and I couldn't find him. I didn't know if he was loved or even alive.

Even in an open adoption, a mother is still separated from her baby. She may not worry about whether her baby is alive and cared for, but she may long to know what's happening day to day in her child's life. Her heart may also be broken.

My friend Diane had a very different experience as a first mom. Her child was also born when she was a teen. She initially wanted to keep her baby, but her mother told her she wouldn't help her raise the child and she would be on her own. For several months she tried to figure out a plan but finally realized she couldn't do it alone. Her aunt and uncle were unable to have children and wanted to adopt, so it made sense to Diane to ask if they would adopt her child.

Her daughter was born by emergency C-section, and Diane didn't see her baby right away. When her aunt arrived at the hospital, the baby was brought to Diane's room for the first time. Her aunt immediately assumed the role of the mother and began caring for the infant. While she was sad, Diane was able to accept this and experienced a sorrowful peace.

After leaving the hospital, Diane and her mother traveled with her aunt and the newborn to the aunt's home state where adoption paperwork was signed. Diane never felt like her baby's mother; she felt more like a cousin. She continued her life always knowing where her daughter was and how she was doing. When the little girl was a year old, Diane did experience anger and regret, but it didn't last long. She continued to feel peace about the decision.

Now more than twenty-five years later, Diane's daughter has a child, and Diane is one of the grandmothers to this little one. She and her daughter have a relationship that sometimes feels like mother and daughter but also fully acknowledges the adoptive parents. Diane also has three more children, and her heart is full. The openness of this kinship adoption has allowed her to have peace and healing from the loss.

In another instance, a first father I'll call Samuel knew absolutely nothing about his child until he received a Facebook message from her adoptive mother. The moment he saw her photo, he knew Alexis was his daughter.

Nearly six years earlier, a woman he didn't know well told him she was pregnant and there was a chance he was the father. Samuel didn't hear from her again until he was asked to sign papers relinquishing his parental rights. He didn't know if he truly was the father, so he asked for a paternity test, but the mother told him her doctor advised against it because it was too risky for the baby. Being young and not knowing what to do, he signed the papers. He didn't even know if the child was a boy or a girl.

Now he had a photo of a little girl who looked like him. Along with her adoptive parents, he agreed to a DNA test that revealed he was her biological father.

In his written account, Samuel says,

> If I'd been able to confirm the baby was mine, I would have kept my child. But not trusting the mother and hearing she had been

with another man, I ended up signing the adoption papers without knowing for sure if she was my daughter. I deeply regret this. I would have kept my child if I'd known she was mine.

He spoke with Alexis for the first time on her sixth birthday. One year later, Jack and Ann, Alexis's adoptive parents, made plans for their families to meet in person.

Our first meeting was marked by a warm exchange of hugs and many unspoken emotions. They invited us to join the family for dinner at a local restaurant, where Alexis and I discovered a shared love of mac and cheese.

The next night Samuel cooked dinner for them at his home. The evening was filled with games and laughter.

I introduced Alexis to the art of playing darts. Her competitive spirit and the way she handled those darts made me realize how similar we are.

And the bond between the families has continued to grow.

As we said goodbye at the end of one visit, Alexis embraced me, uttering these precious words: "I love you." My heart swelled with warmth and joy. Being part of Alexis's life is a blessing and privilege. It is an extraordinary gift given by God to forge a meaningful connection with my daughter.

My journey hasn't been easy. Knowing my child is not living with me is a loss I've had to heal from. I am thankful, though, that she grew up with a very loving family and we have the opportunity for our bond. I am grateful my daughter knows that I love her dearly.

Although they were separated from their children, both Diane and Samuel have peace of mind knowing their children are thriving. In contrast, when I lost my son, I didn't think I

> Cry as much as you need to; it makes sense that you feel so sad. Right now, it feels like you won't survive, but the Lord is with you. He will not let you go.

could survive the unbearable grief. I was so worried about him—I was a mother, and I didn't know where my child was. I nearly lost my mind. I prayed, paced, wrote poems, and talked with people who knew my story, but nothing comforted me.

One day I went to the front of a church for prayer and knelt at the altar. A pastor and some other people laid their hands on me and began praying, but I could not be comforted. I wept and wept. Finally, they shook their heads and walked away. There would be no miracle of physical healing because I wasn't sick. I was devastated by grief. What a difference it would have made if my very real and normal emotions had been acknowledged and empathy expressed.

If I could speak to my young self in those early months, I would wrap my arms around my shaking shoulders and say, "Cry as much as you need to; it makes sense that you feel so sad. Right now, it feels like you won't survive, but the Lord is with you. He will not let you go. Life won't always feel so terrible. Grief takes its time, but little by little, the deepest pain will begin to ease. The Lord has a good plan for your life. Hold on."

Jesus met me in my sorrow. He walked with me through the darkest valley and held me when I thought I would fall apart. He gave me a husband who loved me and grieved with me. And He gave me children to fill my aching arms. I would not have survived were it not for the presence and love of Jesus.

Freedom Prayer for Birth Moms

Please read this entire freedom-giving prayer before praying it. Then pray the parts relevant for you, adding anything you think needs to be included and remembering to engage your heart. Also, of course, use the pronoun that fits your child.

> *Lord, I recognize that I've carried much grief and loss as a birth mother, and today I'm ready to deal with it. But as I prepare to release the pain and emotions of grief and loss, I want to first ask your forgiveness.*

Repent

Lord, please forgive me for the following (select what's applicable to you):

- *all the loss and grief my child feels/felt knowing I gave them up*
- *all resentment or bitterness toward anyone because of my own loss and grief*
- *any resentment or bitterness toward social workers or the adoption agency that worked with me*
- (your additions)

Lord, I choose to receive your forgiveness. (Pause and receive God's forgiveness.) *And based on your forgiveness, I choose to forgive myself.* (Now forgive yourself.)

Forgive Others

Now forgive everyone who contributed to your loss and grief.

Lord, I choose to forgive

- *myself for being in a position where I needed to give up my child*
- *the insensitivity of my social workers for minimizing my pain in my giving up my cherished child*
- *those who expected me to just move on with life as if nothing had happened*

- *my child's adoptive parents for any way they failed or are failing my child as my child deals with their losses*
- (your additions)

Lord, thank you that as I forgive, my heart is being cleansed. Help me continue to forgive as necessary.

Release

If you're a visual person, we encourage you to "see" yourself giving the losses and resulting grief to the Lord or laying them at the foot of His cross.

Lord, I'm ready to release to you the deep sense of loss and grief I've carried over giving up my child. I release the following:
- *the devastating sense of loss I felt in my body, in my emotions, and in my thoughts as I gave up my child*
- *the horrible loss I carried because my arms were empty*
- *the loss I carried because I couldn't know what was happening to my child day by day*
- *the loss I carried because I was forced to give up my hopes and dreams of truly sharing my child's life*
- *the radical loneliness I felt as I grieved alone*
- *the pain of the hypocrisy I felt just going on with life as if nothing had changed*
- *the guilt I felt giving up my child*
- (anything else important to you)

These next bullets apply to open adoption.
- *the anger, resentment, and feelings of being cheated as I watch/watched another family raise my child*
- *the pain of saying goodbye to my child when visiting times are/were over*
- (anything else important to you)

68

Lord, I give you all my grief and loss. Thank you for taking them, and please replace this burden with your peace. Thank you, Lord. In Jesus' name, amen.

ADOPTEE—BETSY

Do you like riding roller coasters? One minute you're climbing high into the air, and the next minute you're descending rapidly.

The emotional life of an adoptee or foster child has a lot of parallels with a roller coaster. It has some predictable emotional highs and lows—especially lows. For example, all day you've been wondering who your birth parents are, and your roller coaster hits bottom. Another day you're down, feeling devastated, because you look so different from the rest of your family.

On the other hand, sometimes you're up. Your adoptive parents, as well as your new family constellation, do love you. You think you'll be okay. But somehow there's still an ache in your heart. There's still an empty place that comes and goes on this roller coaster that's your life.

Mine was a closed adoption, and many of my own ups and downs were unpredictable. I would much rather have felt in control. But I didn't.

I wonder if my first family ever think about me on my birthday. I don't know. Anyway, every time I think about them, I'm down again with my loss. I feel cut off from them. I don't even know who they are or where they live. I have sad days when I just wonder who I am. The emotions seem worse than a headache and a stomachache combined.

Sometimes I feel angry just because. I know it's crazy to be angry, but I don't know who's to blame. I guess I'll just blame everybody. I think I'll kick a hole in the wall.

Have you lost your first family? Do you know how bad it feels?

These messy, painful emotions didn't really hit me until I was six and confronted about my adoption by my little friends. Overwhelming fear shot through me like a dump truck had just unloaded sharp rocks right into the pit of my stomach. Ouch! After this, I was continuously tormented by the haunting feelings of being an outsider, of being different, and of being a nobody going nowhere good.

I am a plan B person, I thought to myself. *Someone given away and later chosen off the adoption "auction block."* I could never change this. I had lost my original family. I could never be a plan A person. A big down.

Confusion grew when I, as a plan B person, was frequently put into a leadership position. I could be leading the line of children into the school library or leading as president of my Brownies troop. But I wondered if the others knew the person they'd selected as leader was a "throwaway kid" who felt both unworthy and incapable of being anyone's leader.

Sometimes, however, I was seated high on my roller coaster. I could see. I could breathe a full breath. I could shout for joy. Let me tell you about one of the highs.

Part of what my adoptive parents did for me was simply taking me places where I could experience God for myself. Such was the case one Easter Sunday morning during my early teen years.

We attended a powerful Easter sunrise service, and in my mind's eye I could see everything the pastor read from the Bible. Wonder and amazement filled me. *Risen! Jesus, you actually came back from the dead, from death to life.* I wanted to laugh and jump and turn cartwheels. I wanted to shake somebody and say, "It's real. It really happened." As the service ended, I had an intense yearning to be alone to savor my thoughts.

"Sure, you can walk home by yourself," my mother said when I asked her. "It's only a few blocks. We'll have breakfast when you get there."

When I was almost home, suddenly, superimposed on my natural surroundings, I saw Jesus hanging on the cross. He was crying and looking toward me. I didn't physically hear words, but I heard them in my spirit. Speaking tenderly to me, He whispered, "I died for you because I love you so very much."

My breath came in quick pants. I felt like I was melting. Every part of my being was fluid, undependable. I trembled as the depth of Jesus' love and the truth of His death for me washed over me, filling me, becoming a reality. This reality was more than a "knowing." It saturated me, penetrated me, and changed me.

Still weak, I looked again. My natural surroundings had returned. There was Mrs. Flegal's house and Mrs. Cummings's. There was the hill and my yard. Everything was the same— except for me. I was not the same! God had just changed the trajectory of my life. He became my anchor. Jesus became very personal for me.

I was quiet at breakfast. It was too soon to share what had happened. It was too sacred.

"I think this is going to be a special Easter," Mother commented as she bustled around the kitchen.

Deep inside, I agreed. For me, it had already been "special." It was the most "up" I had ever felt. After this jubilant Easter vision, when my low times came, I would see Jesus on the cross and hear His life-giving words. My lows never again got as low as before.[3]

I must not bypass one particular low that occurred during my teenage years. My roller coaster felt like it was trying to reach a deep bottom.

My girlfriends and I had all started our periods. The boys in our class were getting taller, and their voices, once squeaky, were positively deeper. Of course, we girls talked about sex and what a strange thing it seemed to be. My Bible clearly explained that sex was reserved for marriage.

Then one day I realized my birth parents probably weren't married. My mom was probably a single mom. That meant I was illegitimate. Nothing could change that fact. I felt frozen, stopped. My deep yearning to be clean, to be right before the Lord, could never be fulfilled. Heartbreak, loss, grief, defilement, and hopelessness filled me. I was inconsolable. Sensing my deep distress, my adoptive parents tried to find out what was wrong, but I couldn't risk telling them.

In the eleventh grade I ran for an office on the student council and lost. How do you think I interpreted this? You're probably right. This was just more evidence. *Now they know how bad I really am. That's why they couldn't vote for me.* My grief poured out for many days.

Was my life one of continuous trauma? No. I had some close friends and a great boyfriend. Naturally athletic, I played tennis and basketball. I was on the debate team. Lots of normal things to do. Awards and honors came my way. My hand received handshakes, awards, and diplomas, but my heart received nothing. Inside, I felt too unworthy.

> My Bible said Jesus came to carry my grief and sorrow, but I didn't know how to give it to Him.

Looking back, I know my adoptive parents had their own poignant losses. Mother lost a baby in the fifth month of her pregnancy. She and my dad never got pregnant again. But I was way too self-absorbed to tune in to their losses and the resulting grief.

I knew God loved me, but I didn't know He could heal my ever-sabotaging grief. My Bible said Jesus came to carry my grief and sorrow (Isaiah 53:4), but I didn't know how to give it to Him. It also said He came to heal the brokenhearted (Luke 4:18 KJV), but possibly like you, I didn't know how to give Him what was in my heart or receive His healing. Although significant healing would eventually come, the constraints of grief would be mine for many years.

Freedom Prayer for Adoptees

Please read this entire freedom-giving prayer before praying it. Then pray the parts relevant for you, adding anything you think needs to be included and remembering to engage your heart.

Lord, I don't want my life defined by being an adopted person. Please help me honestly move through my grief and loss. Empower me so that I may fully embrace my life in a positive new way.

Repent

Please forgive me for the following (select what's applicable to you):

- *all the ways I've hurt other people, especially my adoptive parents, as I struggled with my losses*
- *thinking of myself as a helpless victim*
- *continuing to strive to somehow make myself worthy of being loved*
- *becoming destructive or aggressive as I experienced my loss and grief*
- *thinking negative thoughts about myself even though they don't agree with Scripture*
- *giving up on life and fantasizing about death or making a suicide attempt*
- (your additions)

Lord, I choose to receive your forgiveness. (Pause and receive God's forgiveness.) *And based on Your forgiveness, I choose to forgive myself.* (Now forgive yourself.)

Forgive Others

Now forgive everyone who contributed to your losses and resulting grief.

Lord, I choose to forgive
- *my birth mom for giving me up*
- *my birth mom for my struggles with identity and belonging*
- *my birth mom for feelings of defilement because she wasn't married*
- *myself for my desire to retaliate*
- *my adoptive parents for not always being what I hoped and needed*
- (your additions)

Lord, I thank you that as I repent and forgive, my heart is being cleansed.

Release

If you're a visual person, we encourage you to "see" yourself giving the losses and resulting grief to the Lord or laying them at the foot of His cross.

Lord, I'm willing to release to you the grief I've carried from the major losses in my life. I release the following:
- *the pain of my identity struggles*
- *the pain of feeling like a mistake and not belonging*
- *the pain of feeling defiled because my birth parents weren't married*
- *the anger of being unable to resolve my feelings*
- *the frustration of feeling not good enough or worthy of being loved*
- *my sense of being a helpless victim*
- *my confusion and stress as I try to love two different families who don't always get along*
- (your additions)

Lord, help me see that my identity is in being your child. Please assure my heart that I have a special place in your family that can never be taken away. Thank you today for taking my loss and my grief. In Jesus' name, amen.

FOUR

SHAME AND ISOLATION

As Scripture says, "Anyone who believes in him will never be put to shame." —Romans 10:11

ADOPTIVE MOM—JODI

Shame and isolation will eat you alive. They will swallow you whole. They will take your breath and leave you gasping. The very worst season of my life was as an adoptive mother drowning in shame and isolation.

Our large family was thriving and functioning well. The children were prospering in school and activities, we were active in our local church, we had fun together, and our life seemed like a great and beautiful gift.

Then, slowly, something terrible crept in. One of our children fell into a pit of darkness that we were not equipped to handle. Things spiraled downward and fell apart. Struggles within the family led to disconnection and heartache. Not knowing what else to do, my husband and I made the decision to place our child in residential treatment, straining the already fragile cords of attachment.

It put me into a deep well of shame, feeling like a complete failure. My adoptive mom friends had children who were thriving. Their families seemed full of joy and victory, and we were just pressing through each day like zombies.

To accommodate this child's treatment, this season also included a relocation, taking us away from all that was familiar. Suddenly our ties to our home, our church, and our friends all seemed broken. We huddled together in a new place—a rental—like emotional refugees and wondered if life would ever feel happy again.

I don't remember so many things from that season, but I do remember crying every day. I remember sitting on the corner of a hundred-dollar, secondhand couch every day and weeping. Our contact with our child in treatment was restricted, and I missed that face and that voice beyond reason.

My marriage disintegrated into a shell of going through motions without intimacy. I blamed us as parents for the situation with our child. I believed our parenting was the cause of this crisis, and facing my partner meant facing our shared failure. I just retreated into myself. I felt like I was in a bubble of shame, and I couldn't really reach my hand through the barrier.

How could I go on the way we'd been living? Because our adoptions were of children from another race, our family's story of adoption was visible to anyone who knew us. We'd always celebrated that story. We were proud of our family and our kids. We'd advocated, written a book, been on television. We were passionately on a mission to see more children adopted, and our kids had joined us in this mission.

But then this disaster came, and it felt like we were nothing but frauds. Our own child was no longer in our home, our happy unit no longer existed, and everything felt shattered. We had failed.

At my lowest point, I lost my composure completely. I had a breakdown of sorts. One day I screamed and threw candles at the bedroom door my husband was closing to protect our children from hearing me. One of my adopted daughters came in, comforted me, and picked up the candle pieces. And then I knew I had to get out of that place and not let my children see me like this for one more day. And so I left. I ran away.

By myself, I went to another rental home a missionary friend offered. And I just sat. For days, I just sat. In silence. I begged God to help me. I had no more emotions, no more thoughts, no more hope. I was a stone.

Then suddenly, one day I realized I wasn't alone. Someone was with me in that place as I lay face down on the floor praying. His name was Jesus. He broke through the fog of my shame and started speaking truths to me. I picked up a pen and began writing all the things He was revealing to me.

I wrote and wrote and wrote. And when I was done, everything about our story looked different. I knew I would survive. I knew our family would survive. I saw things I'd never understood. Jesus showed me things only He could reveal.

Do I wish I hadn't fallen to that terrible place of breakdown? I'm not sure, because without it I wouldn't have had the revelations. I wouldn't have surrendered it all to God.

Finally, when I was ready, I returned to my family. I'll never forget that homecoming. My husband had cleaned up the mess I'd made and turned our bedroom into a spa-like retreat, complete with the most luxurious towels—purple, my favorite color. And yes, new candles flickered a beautiful welcome as I entered.

From that experience, I vowed that I would try to use my journey to keep other women from feeling the shame and isolation I'd felt. I had a vision for supporting mothers who have walked in these deep valleys. I understood that I couldn't fix the trauma that tormented my child. Only Christ could do that, and I began to trust Him for it. Shame and isolation tried to rob me of my very life, but Christ stepped in when I was at my lowest point.

And I began being very intentional about having community, deep faithful friendships, that would keep me from being lost again. I knew if I were going to make it as an adoptive parent in the long run, I would need more support. I would need friends who were also fostering and adopting, who understood that the journey could take a troubling turn. I would need others who would pray over me and point me back to God when I lost my way. I would need a safe place to share our struggles in parenting and to confess my shortcomings.

> **Together, we can remind ourselves that God is the author of our children's stories and He will finish writing them in His time. Our job is to stay connected to each other and to Him.**

I committed to finding and cultivating these connections, and it was with these friends that I could face the future, whatever it held. I could share my shame and allow them to reframe it for me out of the well of their faith and shared experiences. And I could do the same for them when they were in the valley. Together, we can remind ourselves that God is the author of our children's stories and He will finish writing them in His time. Our job is to stay connected to each other and to Him.

Freedom Prayer for Adoptive Parents

Please read this entire freedom-giving prayer before praying it. Then pray the parts relevant for you, adding anything you think needs to be included and remembering to engage your heart. Also, of course, use the pronoun that fits your child.

> *Lord, I thank you that you are a God of new beginnings, and today is a new beginning for me. I ask you to empower me as I deal with shame.*

Repent

Please forgive me for the following (select what's applicable to you):

- *for trying to be the perfect parent*
- *for being so quick to blame myself and take on shame and failure when my child isn't doing well*
- *for comparing both my child and my own parenting with others*
- *for any way I've hidden or isolated myself because of my shame/embarrassment*
- *for trying to be self-sufficient and handle everything myself rather than drawing on your help or even connecting with other parents*
- (your additions)

Lord, I choose to receive your forgiveness. (Pause and receive God's forgiveness.) *And based on your forgiveness, I choose to forgive myself.* (Now forgive yourself.)

Forgive Others

Now forgive everyone who contributed to your taking on shame.

Lord, I choose to forgive

- *my child for not accepting my love*
- *my child for not recognizing/appreciating what I've given them*
- *my child for acting out publicly and causing me shame*
- *my spouse for any and all ways they have avoided their part of our responsibility of raising this child*
- *the adoption agency for any way they shamed me*
- (your additions)

*Lord, I've worn a cloak of shame for way too long. Today
I want to begin to remove it, so I choose to declare war on
shame. I'm ready to totally kick it out of my life. Please help
me as I release the shame to you.*

Release

If you're a visual person, we encourage you to "see" yourself
giving the shame to the Lord or laying it at the foot of His cross.

*Lord, I'm ready to release to you the shame and all the ugly
demeaning feelings that go with it. I now release and give
you the following:*

- *any shame around my not conceiving*
- *my failures as a parent*
- *my embarrassment when other adoptive parents' children are doing well and mine is not*
- *my humiliation when my child acts out and others know/
see it*
- *my not being loved or chosen by my adopted child*
- (add any other negative feelings you also need to
release)

*Lord, thank you for taking my pain and shame, and
please help me avoid taking on shame again. As I reach
out to you, give me a fresh strength and courage and fresh
hope. Also, Lord, where I have isolated myself, enable me to
reach out to others to both give and receive support.*

*Thank you for being with me every step of my journey.
In Jesus' name, amen.*

BIRTH MOM—LISA

A few days ago, I was talking with a friend on my phone while
walking on a trail near my house. She began asking questions

about my experience as a first mom, like "How old were you when you had your son?" I found myself hesitant to answer. We talk weekly about vulnerable things, yet this felt more difficult. I felt shame. More than four decades later, I felt shame.

Because circumstances vary widely, I can't speak for all birth mothers. Our experiences are not the same. But over the years as I've connected with other birth mothers whose children were adopted, the dominant emotions I've seen include deep sadness and regret. Anger as well, because many of them were forced to give up their babies or coerced due to no resources or support. But perhaps the most damaging emotion is shame.

Some birth mothers speak of making a courageous and sacrificial decision for their child's sake. They chose life when abortion was readily available. They believed making an adoption plan was the best thing they could do for their child. But shame is magnified for the mother whose children were removed from her, placed in foster care, and later adopted when parental rights were severed. Her inability to be a healthy and safe parent at that time led to tragedy. The deep sense of sorrow, failure, and shame can define a woman.

Regardless of whether a birth mom feels she made a positive choice or that her child was stolen from her, she may experience shame. Some birth mothers have experienced so much trauma that they're stuck in a place that keeps them from healing and moving forward with life. They need compassionate guidance for the healing journey.

Some birth mothers express shame over having sex outside of marriage (if that restriction is part of their faith), shame over an unplanned pregnancy, shame over not keeping their child. Some women don't even tell their future husbands they've given birth and relinquished a child for adoption. They view themselves as tainted.

Author and psychologist Edward Welch writes, "Shame is the deep sense that you are unacceptable because of something you did, something done to you, or something associated with you. You feel exposed and humiliated."[1]

Being a pregnant teen on the cusp of the 1980s was unacceptable in all circles. When I was placed in foster care, I moved from a small logging town in the foothills of Mount Rainier to a large city two hours away. Instead of the four hundred students in my high school at home, my new school had nearly four times that population. Thankfully, this made it easy to disappear in the crowd and disguise my pregnancy with drawstring-waist pants and oversized shirts.

My teachers had a variety of reactions. The choir director said I couldn't sing in the winter concert because it would be disgraceful. In contrast, my Honors English teacher once leaned toward me and quietly said, "This could have happened to me." Her honesty meant the world to me, especially when less kind people had told me, "You made your bed, you lie in it" and "You should have kept your pants on."

I was worried about how I would be treated at the hospital, so I proactively became a volunteer on the postpartum floor. I hoped the nurses would be kinder and less judgmental if they knew me before my baby was born. I wanted them to see me as a smart, capable person and not dismiss me or treat me badly.

While progress has been made, shame seems to be even more prevalent among Christian birth mothers. One mom was sent to a modern-day maternity home, but her parents told the younger siblings she had a mental breakdown and was hospitalized. Another mom was brought home from college and sent to live in the family's guest cottage. Both sets of parents said their presence in the home would be a bad influence on younger siblings.

In the years after Christopher's birth, I struggled with shame over having gotten pregnant, but I was never ashamed of him. I grieved deeply, but I was proud of my beautiful son. New friends couldn't truly understand me if they didn't know about my child. His life had shaped mine so profoundly that it was living a lie to

> Shame runs deep and wide in the hearts of many birth mothers, leading to isolation. But Jesus loves us, and His kind eyes are looking upon us with love.

keep him a secret. So I shared the small number of photos I had of him and told our story to anyone with whom I wanted a meaningful relationship.

Shame runs deep and wide in the hearts of many birth mothers, leading to isolation. The lies of the enemy—*I can never be forgiven, I've ruined God's plan for me, I'll always be a failure,* and *I need to pay for my own sin*—can be loud in our minds. But Jesus loves us, and His kind eyes are looking upon us with love. The truth is louder.

During my pregnancy, the sadness and feelings of abandonment were so extreme that my spirit became more open to God. I felt His presence with me when I was walking to school and when I was alone at night. I was surrounded by Love. Knowing Jesus changed me to the core. I was so transformed by His love that I began to see myself differently.

Freedom Prayer for Birth Moms

Please read this entire freedom-giving prayer before praying it. Then pray the parts relevant for you, adding anything you think needs to be included and remembering to engage your heart. Also, of course, use the pronoun that fits your child.

Lord, I recognize that I've carried much shame as a birth mother, and today I'm ready to deal with it. As I prepare to release the shame, I want to first ask your forgiveness.

Repent
Please forgive me for the following (select what's applicable to you):

- *sex outside of marriage*
- *any way I've contributed to my having to give up my child*
- *trying to hide my past*
- *all the ways I've hurt myself as well as others who cared for me*
- *holding on to shame as well as anger at myself*
- *holding on to anger or bitterness toward those who failed to help me, who caused me to feel trapped or manipulated or worthless*
- *(add anything else that fits for you)*

Lord, I choose to receive your forgiveness. (Pause and receive God's forgiveness.) *And based on your forgiveness, I choose to forgive myself.* (Now forgive yourself.)

Forgive Others

Now forgive everyone who contributed to your taking on shame.

Lord, I choose to forgive
- *my parents for every way they added to my shame*
- *my baby's father for ways he shamed me rather than helping me*
- *the adoption agency for all the ways they shamed me and/or manipulated me to release my baby and/or withheld important information from me*
- *(your additions)*

Lord, I've hidden behind a cloak of shame far too long, and today I want to begin to remove it. I choose to declare war on shame. I'm ready to totally kick it out of my life. Please help me as I release the shame to you.

Release

Lord, I choose to release all shame, embarrassment, humiliation, and pain to you. I also release the following negative emotions (pause and consider each emotion, then truly give the relevant ones to the Lord):

- *regret*
- *sadness*
- *trauma*
- *failure*
- *helplessness*
- *hopelessness*
- *anger*
- *retaliation*
- *self-accusation/blame*
- *desire to hurt myself*
- *desperation, suicide fantasies or attempts*
- (add any other negative emotion relevant to you)

Thank you, Lord, that you are a God of new beginnings. Please wash my slate clean of all shame. I receive that I am righteous in your eyes because you've made me righteous.

Lord, you are the true parent of my child. You knew them from the foundation of the world. You knit them together in my own womb. You made them in an incredible way. You are committed to their life and to the fulfillment of their destiny. Thank you that I can count on you even more than on my child's adoptive parents. You will watch over my child and keep them safe. You always want their best.

Thank you for giving me the courage to birth my child instead of aborting them. Thank you for being with me as I released my child, even though I may not have even been aware of your presence. Thank you for healing my heart and helping me go on with my life.

In Jesus' name I pray, amen.

ADOPTEE—BETSY

Have you ever attempted to remove chipped fingernail polish without the help of polish remover? Frustrating! I've scratched that stubborn polish with my other fingernails, tried to remove it with the tip of my scissors, and with exasperation attempted to file it off with an emery board. No success. Ugly jagged pieces have clung to my nails for dear life.

That's the way shame is; it clings to you for dear life. The difference, however, is that instead of being visible and ugly on the outside, it's invisible and ugly on our inside. Unlike polish applied only to our fingernails, shame covers and shades our entire lives. It's like a dark distorted filter through which we see ourselves and process the experiences of our lives.

"Well, what is shame?" you may ask.

People usually identify their shame as low self-esteem or unworthiness. Our favorite definition is "the sense of being uniquely and fatally flawed." This shame defines who we think we are. It's part of our identity. We might believe there's something terribly wrong with us that can never be fixed.

Before going deeper with shame, another question you may have is "How is guilt different from shame?" Guilt comes from doing or thinking something we know is wrong. We feel guilty. But this guilt doesn't define who we are. Unlike shame, it doesn't define our identity.

An adoptee or foster child is particularly vulnerable to living out of a foundation of shame in at least four ways. First, patterns in our family line often contain a rampant amount of shame as well as sexual sin. Shame is passed down to us. Yes, we have a spiritual inheritance as well as a physical inheritance.[2]

Second, Deuteronomy 23:2 says that an illegitimate person, as well as their descendants, will not be allowed to come into the assembly of the righteous. This curse results in the shame of being an outsider, the shame of not belonging. Like other curses, this curse can be repented of and removed.[3]

Third, shame and trauma are frequently present in the birth mother's life while we're in the womb. Science has now shown that the baby—us—is hugely impacted by the mother's experiences and emotional state.

Fourth, each of us adoptees carries the shame of abandonment. We're not kept by our birth mother, and we feel not wanted or valued. We feel the shame of being worthless as we're placed on the "auction block" for "the whosoever" to choose us. It's important to note that "the whosoever" may be incredibly loving, God-directed people. But that doesn't negate the feelings of shame we carry.

As adoptees, we're all impacted by these four areas of vulnerability even though each of our lives is unique and different from each other.

What is the impact of shame? Because our foundations contain these building blocks of shame, we not only see life through the lens of shame but are uniquely sensitive and more easily devastated as other shaming events occur. Shame is like a double whammy.

One particularly shameful event occurred my junior year in high school. I'd been nominated as secretary for the student council. I was so pleased that I'd been nominated, feeling that winning that position would validate my worth. I also loved the idea of being a decision-maker for the school. Incredibly encouraging, my friends made signs and posters for me.

"You're going to win," they assured me.

"Yes," I said, agreeing as I smiled to myself.

Voting was held one Friday morning in the spring. Announcing the winners would happen at 2:45 p.m., just before the end of the school day. I could hardly wait. This would be my big moment. At last, I'd be able to prove to myself the confidence and value my schoolmates had in me.

I was just getting dressed after physical education class when the announcement came. "We're happy to announce the results of this year's student council election. Lawrence will serve as your new president, Ernie as your new vice president, and Becky G. as your new secretary."

Wait! Something was wrong. The unthinkable had happened. I had lost the election! To me, still struggling with my identity, losing was like a verdict. "You are not worthy," the verdict said, "and they know it."

Holding back tears, I cried inside. The short distance to the school bus seemed like a mile. "Sorry," a couple of kids said casually. Humiliation engulfed me. My heart hurt. The raw-nerve hit would ache for years.

The next year when I graduated from high school, I was awarded several honors. But I could only see myself as "the girl who lost the election."

The good news is that God would heal this debilitating shame—although it would take time and perseverance from me.

> Shame is my enemy. With God's help I will not stop fighting until I have completely kicked this enemy out of my life, including its lies and oppression.

I also saw my parents deal with shame over their child's behavior—my brother's. My dad was head of the Bible department at a local college, and many people went into ministry because of his influence. Yet in our small town, his son was getting arrested, cutting people's clotheslines when he felt like it, and getting a young girl pregnant. Meanwhile, my dad was rubbing elbows with people who'd been targets of my brother's rebellious, hurtful behavior. It takes grace to handle the shame of your child's acting out.

When I realized what an octopus shame had been in my life, I was appalled. Together with my husband, we developed and then spoke out the following declaration: "Shame is my enemy. With God's help I will not stop fighting until I have completely kicked this enemy out of my life, including its lies and oppression."

As I declared war, I first removed the power and influence of my generational family patterns as well as the curse of illegitimacy (Deuteronomy 23:2). (See more about the generational family patterns I discovered in chapter 6.) Next, I addressed my lies. In my healing journey, I found that shame had deceived me into believing many of them. Perhaps you recognize and identify with some of the following:[4]

- *I am the problem.*
- *I'm bad.*
- *If anything goes wrong, it's my fault.*
- *If you knew the real me, you would reject me.*
- *I must wear a mask so people won't find out how horrible I am.*
- *I'm not worthy to receive anything good from God.*

Through prayer, I renounced these lies and replaced them with God's truth. Then I took responsibility for unhealthy and ungodly patterns I had developed. The following list expresses some of them.

- **Blame Shifting:** *I feel better about myself if I put the blame on you.*
- **Isolation/Hiding:** *If you don't know the real me, then you won't reject me. So I'll either wear a mask and pretend to be who you want me to be or just stay away from you.*

- **Perfectionism/Striving:** *If I do everything right, then there's no room for criticism, perhaps you'll accept me, and I might feel more worthy.*

- **Being Overly Apologetic:** *Forgive me for all the ways I'm being a burden to you or offending you. After all, I feel like I was a burden when I was in the womb.*

- **Being Angry and Acting Out:** *I'm angry because I'm victimized and trapped. If I'm already bad at the core, what's the use? I may as well continue to be bad and just prove that truth. I have nothing to lose.*

- **Controlling:** *I'll do what I need to do to keep you from seeing and knowing the real me.*[5]

These patterns, roots, and fruits of shame are not an exhaustive list. Yet they do occur frequently in people living shame-based lives. Do you find yourself in any of these patterns?

Soon I opened my heart to Jesus and asked Him to take the sorrow and heal my wounds from shaming events. Last, I commanded the enemy, who had oppressed me for so long, to leave me in the name of Jesus (Mark 16:17).

It took some time, but I eventually achieved victory over living a shame-based life. The tyranny of shame was broken.

Freedom Prayer for Adoptees

Please read this entire freedom-giving prayer before praying it. Then pray the parts relevant for you, adding anything you think needs to be included and remembering to engage your heart. If you're praying for a child under the age of ten or who lacks the maturity to pray with you, pray over that child while they're sleeping. This is just as effective and can be easier for both of you.

Lord, I thank you that you're a God of new beginnings, and today is a new beginning for me. I ask you to empower me as I deal with shame.

Repent

Please forgive me for the following (select what's applicable to you):

- *any way I've let my shame define who I am and therefore control my decisions*
- *the amount of time I've allowed shame and feeling different/bad to influence my life*
- *being angry with others because I felt shame*
- *becoming passive because of my shame*
- *becoming aggressive and hurting others because of my shame*
- *stressing myself out trying to prove I have worth/value*
- (your additions)

Lord, I choose to receive your forgiveness. (Pause and receive God's forgiveness.) *And based on your forgiveness, I choose to forgive myself.* (Now forgive yourself.)

Forgive Others

Now forgive everyone who contributed to your taking on shame.

Lord, I choose to forgive

- *my parents for the shame of their not wanting/keeping me*
- *the adoption agency for any way they shamed my mom and/or father into giving me up*
- *the adoption agency for all the ways they isolated me and/or shamed me*

- others who have teased/shamed me about being adopted.
- (your additions)

Lord, I've worn a cloak of shame for way too long, and today I want to begin to remove it. I choose to declare war on shame. I'm ready to totally kick it out of my life. Please help me as I release the shame to you.

Release

If you're a visual person, we encourage you to "see" yourself giving the shame to the Lord or laying it at the foot of His cross.

Lord, I'm ready to release to you the shame and all the ugly demeaning feelings that go with it. I release the following:

- *the pain and shame of feeling different because of my adoption*
- *the pain and shame of looking different from my adoptive family and or surrounding culture*
- *the shame of struggling to know who I am*
- *the shame of never feeling good enough*
- *the shame of all the ways I've acted out and hurt myself and others*
- *the stress of having to prove my worth*
- (add any other negative feelings you also need to release)

Lord, I thank you for taking my shame. You've always seen me as good, not shameful, not a mistake, and not second best. Please help me avoid taking on shame again. Help me see myself the way you see me—as one who is righteous and worthy of love and acceptance.

I choose to walk in the fullness of the plans and purposes you have for my life. In Jesus' name, amen.

FIVE

THE IMPACT ON THE FAMILY

The Spirit himself testifies with our spirit that we are God's children. Now if we are children, then we are heirs—heirs of God and co-heirs with Christ, if indeed we share in his sufferings in order that we may also share in his glory. —Romans 8:16–17

ADOPTIVE MOM—JODI

My biological daughter turned toward me from the corner of the sectional she sat on, her eyes full of tears. We'd been talking about her younger adopted brother and his concerning struggles, and I'd pushed the conversation too far. As she looked at me with anguish, I was again reminded that struggles in our family don't just happen to the parent. They happen to the entire family unit.

One of the points of challenge that must be faced and accepted is that foster care and adoption will touch everyone in the family. Everyone—grandparents, aunts, uncles, extended family, and even close friends—will be impacted by the decision to open our hearts and doors to foster care and adoption. Siblings will particularly have their lives changed by this experience.

"How will this impact my biological child?" is a question asked by many potential foster and adoptive parents. Growing up in a family that chooses foster care and adoption will stretch everyone in the family constellation. Children will see their parents living out the call to this journey and will also have an opportunity to witness the faithfulness of their parents in responding with love to challenges. And children see that parents are willing to stretch themselves to bring beauty and redemption to a vulnerable child's life.

I'll never forget when my biological, college-aged daughter served on a panel of young people in adoptive families at a major conference. A member of the audience asked, "I'm afraid if I adopt, my biological kids may suffer. What is your advice?"

My daughter looked at her squarely and said, "Remember, your role as a parent is not to give your children a perfect life. It's to make them more like Jesus."

> Everyone—grandparents, aunts, uncles, extended family, and even close friends—will be impacted by the decision to open our hearts and doors to foster care and adoption.

I could not have been prouder of her at that moment.

I know this child has been through a complex, often challenging, and sometimes painful road along with her parents as some of her adopted siblings have struggled. Yet I also know she would do anything for her siblings and adores each of them. Rather than speak for her, we've asked her to share a few reflections with you here.

SIBLING IN ADOPTIVE FAMILY—MACKENZIE

Adoption impacts the entire family. Maybe you treasure biological children and wonder how they will love a child from a different background. Maybe you're afraid how it will affect them, what they'll be exposed to, or how they'll adapt. All those fears are valid and will become relevant at some point in the story. Biological children make sacrifices in adoption, just as parents do. Yet the moments of growth and tremendous joy far outweigh the challenges. Those are the moments the family works together, and it starts with honoring your biological child's crucial role in knitting their new siblings into the family unit.

Our first adoption happened when I was three years old. My parents gave me a Black baby doll with deep dark skin and big brown eyes and explained that my new baby sister would look like her. How exciting! But I was confused when they brought home the "wrong one"—a tiny biracial baby with tan skin and sparkling green eyes. While she didn't quite match my dolly, I accepted her and adored her the moment I laid eyes on her. I was just so excited to have a baby sister that my mom had to prevent me from suffocating her with squeezes. I thought she was the cutest little thing in the world.

Our next adoption happened much later, when I was entering high school. When my parents proposed the idea of adding children from Uganda to our family, I was elated. I was a young Christian starting to become aware of inequalities in the world and how fortunate I was to have my needs met. That's perhaps the first important lesson I learned—unless the child is extremely young, adoption should not be their first exposure to real-life issues. If children are instilled with a sense of gratitude for their blessings, it will be easier for them to understand sharing those blessings with new children.

I also credit my parents for asking what I thought about this adoption. They genuinely wanted my input and involvement. This was so important for me, and I think it's important for any biological child. Even toddlers can be included in the process of preparing the family home for adoption, like picking out a stuffed animal for their new sibling or giving them a tour of the house when they arrive. Special roles make memories and help biological kids feel included. I felt empowered in our adoptions, even visiting Uganda to meet my siblings in their home environment so I could better understand them. I also felt very secure in my parents' love and commitment to me, so I never once questioned that or felt threatened. Your biological child needs to be in a place of deep confidence in your relationship in order to feel safe "sharing" you with someone new.

Once the adoption took place, we experienced an expected awkward transition for everyone. A few months into being home with my new siblings, I thought, *Wow. I don't know how to get used to this!* I felt welcoming toward them, curious about them, and fond of them, but their presence challenged all my norms and comforts. It was a lot to process.

Another aspect of having adopted siblings was my life being really different from my friends' lives. This was especially true because our adoption was obvious—my appearance doesn't match my siblings. Because I'm White and all my siblings are Brown or Black, every place we enter invites curiosity, questions, and even moments of outright prejudice.

People I barely know have asked me extremely insensitive questions my whole life, such as how my siblings' parents died or why they couldn't care for them. I've also had to witness my siblings being profiled and disrespected in public places due to the racism still present in our country. Nevertheless, these experiences taught me a level of compassion as well as an interest in racial justice and equality that I would not have developed otherwise.

Growing up with adopted siblings forced my exposure to some hard realities. No matter how closely my parents sheltered us, adoption reveals the suffering at the core of the human experience. I heard about morally mature themes: abandonment, poverty, abuse, neglect, addiction. Even when I was a toddler, my parents explained my sister's adoption to me in the simplest terms. They were age-appropriate, but there's a shock and loss of innocence in understanding that some mommies and daddies cannot (or will not) take care of their babies. To understand on even a basic level that your siblings are adopted is to also understand that there is tremendous pain and lack in the world. I witnessed a lot of suffering in the people I call family.

That exposure, however, profoundly shaped who I am today. I am a therapist by profession, and I do believe my unique family constellation contributed to my interest in human issues and my passion for healing. Awareness is not a bad thing. But exposure to pain is a form of emotional weight that has to be managed tenderly within the adoptive family.

Beyond these tough adjustments, adoption brought so many incredible things into my life. It introduces beautiful variety to the ordinary. Besides being some of my best friends, my siblings are my teachers. They're each a unique treasure who has expanded my world and awareness. Adoption helped me develop social and emotional maturity and gave me countless tools for connecting with all types of people in the workplace and my personal life.

Adoption has also shaped me spiritually, as the many storms my family weathered forced me to cling more closely to God. Growing up in a diverse family made me more culturally proficient and more loving and open to people of all stories. I can't imagine any more valuable gift than this.

Adoption is a lifelong story of grace. I realized early on in our family's journey that challenges can either "make you bitter or make you better." I had to have grace for my parents as they learned to love new children and faced setbacks they weren't prepared for. I had to have grace for my siblings as they healed from deep losses, which at times created challenging behaviors or dynamics between us. I had to have grace for myself as I navigated the constant ups and downs and sometimes acted out of frustration. Moments of pain are inevitable in the adoptive family, but as we continue to walk in grace, the patience and love and gratitude we have for one another is always growing.

I believe if a family is called to adopt, biological children will also be called—and we can trust God's generous grace to carry us through any uncertainty we'll face. The way adoption changed me for the better cannot be measured. And the bonds I have with my siblings cannot be measured. I am so very grateful for God's work in my life through my siblings.

Freedom Prayer for Siblings

Please read this entire freedom-giving prayer before praying it. Then pray the parts relevant for you, adding anything you think needs to be included and remembering to engage your heart. If you're praying for a child under the age of ten or who lacks the maturity to pray with you, pray over that child while they're sleeping. This is just as effective and can be easier for both of you.

> *Lord, thank you for the gift of adoption. Thank you that my adopted sibling was placed in my life for a divine purpose. Help me appreciate the ways having this sibling has made my life richer and impacted me in many positive ways. Help me see my sibling the way you see them and love them the way you love them. Show me how I've grown and matured through our family's adoption challenges.*

Repent

> *I ask you to forgive me for the times I've rejected my adopted sibling and shut them out of my heart. Forgive me, too, for those times I've resented having to share my space, my belongings, or my parents' love and time with them. Please forgive me for any judgments I've held against them, and*

give me a heart of compassion instead. (Pause to receive God's forgiveness. Then based on His forgiveness, also forgive yourself.)

Forgive Others

Lord, today I choose to forgive my adopted sibling for any way they've caused me or my family pain turmoil, crisis, or division. I want to let go of the anger or criticism I carry. I let go of the need to rescue or control my sibling as I trust you with their life. I also want to let go of the judgments I've made toward my parents when they didn't seem to handle things the right way. I want to give all this to you. (Pause to release these things to the Lord.)

Release

Thank you for lifting these things out of my life and for bringing me your peace as I continue to release them to you. Please continue to restore our family to true unity through the power of your love and by your Holy Spirit. In Jesus' name, amen.

PART TWO

SEEKING HEALING

Are you ready for more? Follow along as we continue to share not only our pain and insights but also how God entered our stories and we each began a healing journey. We invite you to experience how we faced our own pain and began to confront the lies we were deceived into believing. We each began to trust God to heal the deep wounds of our heart as well as those of our adopted children.

It's been an eye-opener for us individually to see that we have a real enemy the Bible calls the devil and Satan—an enemy who takes advantage of the weak and vulnerable places in our lives. The Bible says, "Your adversary, the devil, prowls around like a roaring lion, seeking someone to devour" (1 Peter 5:8 NASB). The good news you can go to the bank with is that God's Word totally assures us that we have authority over our enemy and protection from his kingdom (Luke 10:19). We don't have to allow the devil to find us to devour!

Come join us and explore your own life as we share ours. You're invited to be freshly empowered as you share in the Freedom Prayers at the end of each segment.

Receive now, in his own words, how one adoptee sought healing from his trauma and found deep recovery.

ADOPTEE—TRENT

Almost everyone I know has a scar. Each scar is a permanent reminder of something terrible that happened. Each scar has a story. Not all scars serve as a reminder of physical pain. Many of us also carry emotional scars. Although emotional scars aren't visible, they also tell a story. For many years, I considered myself broken, damaged, and scarred beyond repair.

I was born into a family filled with extreme dysfunction. My earliest years were filled with domestic violence, severe neglect, and extensive sexual abuse. I find it difficult to adequately describe the pain and suffering I endured. After a few very traumatic years, I was taken into the foster care system at the age of four. Fear dominated my existence as I traveled through five different homes. I cried myself to sleep each night and prayed for a family to call my own.

Then when I was nine, my prayers were answered. My biological brother and I were adopted by two people who are now my mom and dad in every sense of the word. I wish I could tell you that love was enough to provide healing, but early trauma changes who you are. You can either let it take you or decide to fight it. I was determined to fight it.

Although facing my trauma was the most challenging part of my life, I was able to come to dramatic levels of healing. My adoptive family led me to the ultimate healing that's found only in God. As I found my new identity in Christ, I decided I was not a victim nor damaged goods. Over time, I identified as a strong

Christian young man, devoted to God, dedicated to family, and devoted to using my painful past to help others.

As I found true healing in God, He transformed my thinking. I began to view my scars as a sign that while deep pain had occurred, so had healing. As a result, I've taken the painful experiences from my past and used them to bring glory to God.

I give God all the glory for my healing, and I'm thankful for the scars.

SIX

FACING THE UNKNOWN

You will know the truth, and the truth will set you free. —John 8:32

ADOPTIVE MOM—JODI

I was overseas on ministry work when I received a late-night call from my husband. "Our daughter is upstairs crying. What should I do?"

He told me she'd discovered her half sister, being raised in another country, uses the same month, day, and year for a birthday. After checking with some relatives, our daughter was told that her documents had been falsified during the adoption process to make her look younger.

She was devastated to learn this news. This brought into question everything she understood about herself, her age, and her place as the "baby girl" in our family.

Walking into a foster care or adoption story is a faith walk with an abundance of unknowns. Truth in adoption stories can be illusive, and facing the unknown is part of the experience. I hardly know a person in foster care or adoption who doesn't feel like they were given incomplete information about the child they agreed to parent. But truth is so important, isn't it? Without truth, how can we know how best to love and nurture our children?

Facing the unknown with your foster and adopted children is a journey that happens over time, not all at once. A child who's experienced the loss of their parents has already suffered. This is true whether the loss happened at birth or many years later. So facing the facts of that truth has to be entered into with great care and wisdom. A young child may not be ready to shoulder the burden of all the circumstances that led to their separation from family; some facts in a child's story can be terribly heavy. We must encourage our children to pursue knowing their story and facing the truth, but it's wise to choose a time when they have the maturity and ego strength to walk into those realities.

Small children need the freedom to live in joy and experience childhood without added heaviness. This is such a tricky balancing act in an adoptive family. Each child comes to us with a set of facts, a story of brokenness on the part of their biological family. Every foster and adoptive parent must wrestle with how and when to face this truth with their child.

In our family, we chose to let the children take the lead. We answered questions they posed to us about their adoption or biological family, but we didn't give them additional information until they were of an age when we felt the heaviness of that truth could be carried. Generally, we felt they could process these hard truths in the later teen years. Some recommend that a child should know everything by the age of twelve, but each child is unique, and a parent knows a child's heart and readiness best.

It's important to honor your child's family of origin. You don't have to agree with the birth family's lifestyle or choices. You can simply honor your children's birth parents by speaking positive words about them. Acknowledging that they chose to give your child life and anything else you can add to speak positively will be helpful to your children. So be sure your heart attitude mirrors how the Lord sees the birth family.

Fostered and adopted children often hold fantasies of what their biological family or parents may be like. Facing their actual stories can sometimes crush these fantasies, and a new story has to be written in their souls. Often during this season of facing the unknowns, the child will pull away from the second parents. They're on their own journey of discovery and wrestling with many issues internally. They're leaning toward their past and trying to feel more connected to their biological family as a way to establish identity. This can be hard on the second parents, but it's a necessary journey for all.

You don't have to agree with the birth family's lifestyle or choices. You can simply honor your children's birth parents by speaking positive words about them.

For the adoptee, disappointments in what they imagined versus reality must be faced, and this can be hard to process. While some stories of reconnection with the birth family are beautiful and redemptive, not all stories go this way. They don't all have a fairy tale ending. Sometimes the birth parent doesn't want the reconciliation and reconnection the child seeks. Sometimes the birth family is unwelcoming and unkind. And sometimes the brokenness of the first family's life circumstances hasn't improved and the need for the child's removal is on full display. When this occurs, it can be a crushing blow to the idealized fantasies the child has carried.

Who among us could live up to a child's fantasy that we're perfect and will heal all their loss of the past? Certainly, all families, both biological and adoptive, have challenges. So in these seasons of birth family reconnection, there's struggle and wrestling within the child to deal with so many feelings. It's common for adopted children to discover they have full or half siblings born to their birth parents. And these relationships must also be navigated. The child is faced with creating a new story that embraces brokenness and truth but still feels beautiful.

It's a fortunate instance where the relationship with birth parents and adoptive parents can be integrated. While this is always the goal, the complexities are many for all involved. God's design is that we have a primary attachment to one mother figure and one father figure. It's hard enough to have a successful relationship with one set of parents, isn't it?

As my adopted children became young adults, we tried to give them complete freedom to explore birth family relationships at their own pace and comfort level. But in their younger years, we kept their lives simpler and focused on their connection to us and our family as a "second" family while always acknowledging and honoring the reality of their family of origin. We shared biological family photos in our home and maintained connection with extended family if these relationships already existed (as in the case of older child adoption). But we also felt intensely protective of our children, wanting to shield them from some of the harder truths we knew about their families of origin that led to the need for adoption.

I adore my children, and I wanted them to heal and be strong in their identities before facing the traumas of the past that fractured their birth family. While protecting them while young, I was also intentional about keeping myself informed about their birth family in whatever way possible. Social media and the internet give us lots of opportunities for this from afar. Where relationships existed with extended family, we were intentional to connect our children to grandparents or other relatives once we understood that these relationships were safe for the child.

And this is where facing the unknown is so important. In adoption, there's a tendency to enter into parenting as if the child's life begins at adoption. Not only is this untrue, but that attitude is filled with negative consequences for the child.

I had to face the truth that all my children had a history before I adopted them—even a prenatal history. Every child has a genetic history and a spiritual history, and every aspect of our life comes to bear in shaping who we are. I grew tenacious to learn everything I could about my children and their families of origin. In the case of my internationally adopted children, I found relatives, hired translators, and went to great lengths to piece together their story, making the trip to meet many individuals in the family. I dug into the story.

I wanted to know the truth so I could, as much as possible, help piece together the whole truth for my daughter. A commonly quoted Scripture is "You will know the truth, and the truth will set you free" (John 8:32). Any of us who's lived in a family of secrets knows they become like a cancer, as do unanswered questions. They grow and trouble us with doubt and questioning. We're not free but bound by these secrets and unanswered questions. I didn't want any secrets to have power over my child, but I also didn't want to expose her to hard truths before she was ready.

This is the tightrope adoptive parents must walk along, balancing the freedom of the truth with giving their child the chance to grow without so much heaviness. After much prayer for discernment and the advice of counselors, when my children seemed ready, I wanted them to know every truth. Because only in this truth could they really be free.

Freedom Prayer for Adoptive Parents

Please read this entire freedom-giving prayer before praying it. Then pray the parts relevant for you, adding anything you think needs to be included and remembering to engage your heart. Also, of course, use the pronoun that fits your child.

Lord, I need your help. First Corinthians 10:13 tells me you will not give me more than I can bear, but I feel as if I've hit a wall. I've exhausted my faith to believe my child will get better. I've run out of wisdom as I try to answer their questions. I'm struggling to handle their ongoing problems.

As my child faces the fact that their first family was broken, I need your wisdom to evaluate their maturity and ego strength so I know how much information to share and the right words to use. Guide me as I help them process the difficult facts of their life.

Anytime my child withdraws from our family and needs space to connect with their birth family or process their identity, please help me see that their withdrawal is not about me but about their wounding. Lord, thank you for healing my sense of rejection.

I call upon you now to help me see beyond today. I know from Romans 15:13 that you are the God of all hope. Please give me a download of fresh hope about my child's life and my ability to help them build their life on the secure foundation of your love for them.

Empower me afresh in your love. In Jesus' name, amen.

BIRTH MOM—LISA

The loneliness and isolation during my pregnancy brought me to a desperate place, and I was yearning for rescue. I hoped my aunt would one day drive up next to me while I was walking to school and tell me I could live with her family—that they would help us. I dreamed of family friends we'd visited just a year before opening their home to me. I imagined coming out of school one afternoon to find them waiting in the parking lot ready to help me pack my belongings and leave this life for something so much better.

Rescue did come, but not in the form I imagined.

I found my thoughts drifting to God more and more often, especially at night when the day grew quiet and I lay in bed. I'd been raised to know God, but without knowing Him in a deep and personal way, prayers I'd memorized didn't yet hold deep meaning for me.

Alone, I immersed myself in my studies and stayed after school each day to study at a table in the counseling center until the janitor needed me to leave. That same table was a safe place for me during school events like pep assemblies, which held no importance to me. Typical high school activities seemed trite and ridiculous for a girl who was carrying a baby all by herself.

A girl in my philosophy class was kind to me and became my friend. Linda was the only person who invited me to her home during those long months of isolation. I had dinner with her family and went to a church youth group—a new experience for me. Linda also gave me my first Bible, a paperback *Living Bible New Testament and Psalms*. On the inside cover, she wrote, *There is a friend who is closer to you than a brother*, which comes from Proverbs 18:24. She told me Jesus loved me.

Could He love me? Did He have answers for this mess of a life? I couldn't imagine. But I began seeing Jesus in a new way. He became real and alive to me. He was by my side walking through the darkest valley of my life. He was my Good Shepherd who guided and protected me. When I felt completely alone in the world and filled with fear, He was with me.

After I was separated from my son, the unknowns were incredibly hard. I didn't know where my child was. I didn't know if Christopher was sad or scared or loved. I knew virtually nothing about his adoptive parents. I believed they were thrilled, though. It was January of a brand-new year, and they had a baby in their arms. Their longing was fulfilled. But I was in agony.

I knew Jesus now, and I had a newfound hope in the power of prayer, so I prayed for my son and his parents. I prayed blessings over them and asked the Lord to give them wisdom and strength. I knew if Jesus could be with me, He could also be with Christopher and his family. I prayed they knew and loved the Lord like I did. I had never met them, but I loved them.

Over the years, the sorrow eased, but Mother's Day and Christopher's birthday were the hardest days of the year. My husband, Russ, witnessed the depth of my sadness and held me as I wept. Giving birth to our baby girl eight years later filled my arms and my heart with gratitude but didn't instantly reverse the sorrow of losing my son.

Most often I prayed with tears, but sometimes I was filled with anger at the injustice of what happened to me and many other birth mothers I came to know. One mom, Stacy, shared her story of being sent to a maternity home in 1975 with the plan that her son would be placed for adoption. As his birth grew near, she realized she couldn't give him up and wanted to raise him. When she told her caseworker of her decision, Stacy was informed that she could keep her baby, but she would have to pay the bill for her five-month stay. This was impossible. With no money and no hope, she was forced to go through with the adoption.

No ethical agency would do something like this now, but manipulation and coercion are still used. Even though women have many more options for open adoption and information about adoptive families, the balance of power still doesn't lean toward the vulnerable mother trying to sort out her options. Manipulation and fear can still drive life-altering decisions.

When a mom has more control and can make an informed decision, she has more influence over the adoption plan. Often this includes a degree of openness with the adoptive parents. The range of experiences is so vast that it's hard to speak to every possibility, but I know moms who have more peace than I had.

My heart breaks for moms in countries with extreme poverty who have no option but to place their child in an orphanage. It's literally a matter of life and death. This is the case with many of the internationally adopted children and adults I know. Devastating problems with this situation go far beyond the scope of this book, but I think of these mothers who may not even know where in this big world their child lives and whether they're loved.

If you are a first or birth mom and share my love for God, you've prayed your heart out through many long nights. Maybe you've cried out to Jesus in despair or even anger. How could this have happened? How could your child be in the arms of another mother?

At least one-third of the psalms express thoughts of sorrow, disillusionment, despair, and even anger. These are called psalms of lament. Lament is defined as "a passionate or demonstrative expression of grief."[1] *Merriam-Webster* defines it as "to mourn aloud: wail."[2]

In his book *Dark Clouds, Deep Mercy*, Mark Vroegop writes, "Lament typically asks at least two questions: (1) 'Where are you, God?' (2) 'If you love me, why is this happening?'"[3] In lament, we may feel alone and wonder how we could be suffering this loss if God truly loved us.

In lament, we pour out our hearts to God without holding back. We turn toward Him in our sorrow, not away. We can lament because we hold to the truth that God is good and we're safe with Him. In Psalm 62:8, David writes, "Trust in him at all times, you people; pour out your hearts to him, for God is our refuge."

I assure you, our good Father can handle our honest emotions. We don't need to hold back to be "good" Christians; we can be honest Christians. To pray in the midst of our sorrow is an act of faith. We're not running from God but into His arms, where we find safety. And when we don't understand, we lean harder into Him.

When the child you love is far from you, separated by miles or even continents, God is near. We can lament the distance, our inability to hold our child close to our heart and kiss the top of their sweet head. In the same breath we can trust the Lord to embrace and protect them, believing that one day, in this life or the next, we will see the goodness of God in this story.

> **To pray in the midst of our sorrow is an act of faith. We're not running from God but into His arms, where we find safety.**

Mark Vroegop also writes, "In all we feel and all the questions we have, there comes a point where we must call to mind what we know to be true."[4] We reflect on the ways God has been trustworthy and good to us. We consider the great love Jesus showed us when He chose to go to the cross. While our hearts may be breaking, we can put our trust in Him.

This is the story of my life. I will always be sad that I lost my son to adoption—and sometimes I'll be angry. This is also true about my daughter we lost in a car accident. I will always be sad, and sometimes I'll wonder why us, why on that day, and why that curve in the highway. I pour my heart out to the Lord knowing all the while He is my refuge. I trust Him with my life and with my children. I call to mind the truth that He is good and His love is better than life.

Psalm 73:25–26 in the Christian Standard Bible says:

> Who do I have in heaven but you?
> And I desire nothing on earth but you.
> My flesh and my heart may fail,
> but God is the strength of my heart,
> my portion forever.

Freedom Prayer for Birth Moms

Note that you can choose which of the following two prayers to pray according to your situation. Please read the entire freedom-giving prayer you select before praying it. Then pray the parts relevant for you, adding anything you think needs to be included and remembering to engage your heart. Also, of course, use the pronoun that fits your child.

Prayer for Open Adoption

Lord, this open adoption is/was harder than I expected. Sometimes I resent my child's adoptive parents for being able to provide for them in ways I cannot/could not. Sometimes I feel critical and bitter because I see their weaknesses. Sometimes I feel I'm in competition for my child's love.

I confess these negative attitudes and feelings. They're wrong, and I'm tired of struggling with them. I want to give them all to you today. (Pause and give your negative feelings to the Lord.)

Lord, please help me accept the things I cannot change. Give me an appreciation for those ways my child's parents are loving and providing for them. Give me your perspective on these years of my child's life that I might see the situation in a whole new light. Thank you for your help.

As you bring your healing, let the fullness of your abundant love continue to fill the hole in my heart until I am completely healed. In Jesus' name, amen.

Prayer for Closed Adoption

Lord, it's so hard not knowing where my child is or who is parenting them. Are they keeping them safe? Are they loved? Lord, I give you the pain of my thousands of unanswered questions. It breaks my heart not to know how my child is. I especially need your help on their birthday and some holidays.

I bring my deep sense of missing them to you. Please watch over them. Give my child the love I wish I could be giving to them. Let them be well taken care of. Please be there for them through every difficult time. Help my child come to know you at an early age and learn to put their trust in you.

Lord, as I continue to choose to commit the care of my child's life to you, I depend on you to continue to give me your peace. In Jesus' name, amen.

ADOPTEE—BETSY

There we both were in the Norfolk airport, birth mom and daughter holding up signs. Mine said "Betsy," hers "Virginia." We weren't sure we would be able to recognize each other, because this was our first face-to-face meeting. Frankly, I was terrified. What if we didn't even like each other?

I spotted Virginia through the crowd. She was about my height with brown eyes and soft fine hair like mine. Lowering our signs, we spontaneously ran toward each other and hugged—a long happy hug. Even in my most optimistic fantasies, I wasn't sure this moment would ever happen.

Although I deeply loved my adoptive parents, there was still a yearning in me to understand who I was more completely, to understand my roots. The "FBI agent" in me rose up looking for clues to my unanswered questions. *How am I like Virginia? How am I different? How much did giving birth to me cause her major problems?* And then, a question every adoptee asks: *Did my birth mom really love me and want to keep me but was forced to give me up?*

Sitting at the table in her home a few hours later, I noticed the words on her teacup: "Granny on the go." Now, that was certainly like me. As I listened to her stories relating to family and friends, I realized, *Oh my goodness, she's an untrained counselor to them.* Counseling was my profession! Later that evening, after preparing for bed, I returned to the kitchen for a cup of water. Virginia was there too. We were wearing identical pink nightgowns! We looked at each other and laughed. I felt overwhelmed by our commonalities.

The next day held even more surprises. I was showing Virginia photos from each decade of my life when I came to one of me playing the banjo. My love for this instrument had never made much sense to me since my adoptive parents raised me with classical music. Sometimes, however, I had an insatiable desire to hear a good rendition of "Foggy Mountain Breakdown."

Tears rose up in Virginia's eyes. "My father was the best banjo player in our entire county!" she exclaimed. "As a child, I never went to bed without hearing a good banjo tune. He played every night."

My mystery was solved. I must have heard him play while I was in Virginia's womb, or maybe banjo music was just in my birth family's DNA! As she continued introducing me to the unknown parts of my life, some of my questions finally had answers.

The next unknown Virginia shared with me was around a dramatic turning point in both of our lives. The atmosphere around us changed, as she looked quite sober and began to speak almost in a whisper. These are her words as best as I remember:

The week my parents found out I was pregnant, my father determined to put an end to what he called my "problem." He made arrangements with a doctor who was willing to perform an abortion even though it was illegal.

We arrived at the doctor's office around 7:00 a.m. that unforgettable morning. I can still feel how cold it was in the dark. I was shaking all over. Dad got out of our truck and signaled for me to follow. Before I could move, however, I heard a loud voice that said, "Don't do it. Two wrongs don't make a right!"

Quickly, I looked behind me to see who was speaking. But to my great surprise, no one was there. Then, suddenly, I just knew. I knew it was the Lord who had spoken to me. Peace came over me. My shaking began to stop. I knew with all my heart that I was not to have this abortion. It was settled.

I locked the doors of our truck and refused to get out. Even when my father and the doctor got mad and pleaded with me, I still said no. Looking back, I don't know how I did it. I guess the Lord must have helped me.

Trying to take it all in, I listened in silence. I literally had been minutes away from being killed when the voice of the Lord and Virginia's daring obedience spared my life. Simultaneously, shock, gratitude, and deep questions overwhelmed me.

Virginia and I reached across the table and took each other's hands. I was looking at a woman who at her own expense had chosen to give me life. Suddenly I saw her in a new light. This courageous teenager had listened to God and faced the wrath of two adult authority figures in order to save my life.

"Thank you," I said again and again. "How can I ever thank you enough?" Through this miraculous story, more dots of my life became connected.

"Oh," I reflected, "perhaps this explains the tremendous fear of death that's tormented me all my life. I really had been so close to dying."

This tender, unexpected revelation Virginia shared was one of the profound moments of our new relationship. Its effects are still reverberating in my life even as I write this.

Over the next two days, my weekend with Virginia alternated between treasures of information and points of questioning. For example, finding her created an issue I should have anticipated but didn't. *Where does she fit into my life? What category should*

I put her in? I didn't need another mother. I already had one I'd adored for fifty-three years. Virginia, however, wasn't "just a friend" either, because she'd given me the precious gift of life. I wrestled with different ideas until I came up with a unique category: birth mother, life giver. That's how I would think of her.

Open and closed adoptions both have advantages and disadvantages. But when I think of trying to form that new relationship into a category that fits, my heart goes out to children of open adoption who are forced to develop a conceptual framework that fits both families, both worlds. And, of course, this dilemma is only intensified for foster children. There are, however, some advantages to the adopted child knowing the realities of their first family, even if brokenness is apparent.

One of the unknowns I was searching for was generational patterns. Generational patterns, both good and bad, might be affecting me. Was there abuse, addiction, imprisonment, mental health issues, anger, or sexual sin in Virginia's life and her family line? Had anything gone wrong in the area of business or in handling money? What about my birth father? Who was he? What kinds of patterns were in his generational line? With a queasiness in my stomach, I listened intently, trying not to ask too many questions as Virginia risked pouring out her life story.

> Generational patterns, both good and bad, might be affecting me.

I quickly recognized shame and the resulting intimidation. Next came the significant pattern of sexual sin. For example, in Virginia's generation, two children were born of unmarried moms, me being one of those children. The next generation had four. She mentioned five in her grandchildren's generation. My heart grew heavy with this news.

I could see both the positive and negative inheritance in myself. On the negative side, as I also observed in my newly found birth mother, I saw lots of shame, control, intimidation, fear, and sexual sin. God was about to give me His way out of these pressures to sin that had pervaded my thought life and emotions.

I felt the tearing ache of internal conflict. I wanted to know more, but I didn't. The Holy Spirit, however, began connecting the dots for me. Sinful generational patterns opened the door for the enemy's torment. That's why I started having uncontrollable sexual fantasies at age five. They went way beyond the normal childhood sexual curiosity. For example, as I shared in an earlier chapter, I would visualize people I passed on the street as totally naked. Soul torment! I felt dirty and defiled, way too ashamed to tell anybody. I tried hard to stop it, but with little success. (You'll find prayers on breaking generational patterns in chapter 12.)

My weekend with Virginia was one of the most significant times of my life. By the end of my stay, I had a much greater understanding of myself. I had thought about Virginia and her family line, as well as about my adoptive parents and my grandparents who had loved me so well. I was facing the fact that I had inherited significant positives and negatives from each of these generational lines. Both had played a major role in the formation of my identity. So much to think about.

Leaving, I had a new desire to help Virginia overcome her issues, some of which I could now see had developed because of my birth. As I said, I recognized shame, the signs of shame I knew so well. One was that she looked down at the floor as she walked. I also noticed her extreme desire to please others.

I cried out, *Lord, please give me an opportunity to help Virginia get rid of the crippling effect of shame in her life, the shame she carries because of me.* Keep reading to learn how He was to do just that!

In the weeks that followed my visit, I realized I'd been trying to determine my identity from my two human families rather than from God. God, my creator, knew me from the beginning of time and had a specific plan and purpose for my life (Jeremiah 29:11). I had been defining myself way too narrowly, way too much from the physical point of view. Yes, my two families are incredibly important, but Father God is more important. He has known me from the very beginning and will know me into eternity.

Little by little, I made this crucial shift to seeing, feeling, and experiencing God as my most important parent. And as I did, I entered a deeper realm of reality.

As an adoptive parent, you can give this revelation of God as Father to your child. This is an incredible gift that will help greatly accelerate your child's emotional growth and stability.

Freedom Prayer for Adoptees

Please read this entire freedom-giving prayer before praying it. Then pray the parts relevant for you, adding anything you think needs to be included and remembering to engage your heart. If you're praying for a child under the age of ten or who lacks the maturity to pray with you, pray over that child while they're sleeping. This is just as effective and can be easier for both of you.

> *Lord, John 8:31–32 tells me that knowing the truth brings me freedom. Sometimes the truth has been ugly and hard to hear. Forgive me for all the ways I've run away from dealing with it. Give me courage to face and process the unknowns about both of my families. I do thank you for the times the unknown turned out to be helpful and good and gave me confidence.*
>
> *Please help me find a place to put each family both in my mind and in my heart. I need huge amounts of your grace to navigate between them.*
>
> *As I learn things I don't like about my birth family, give me the ability to forgive and release them. It's not my place*

to judge them. Help me realize that these facts don't define who I am. Let me come to love what is good about my birth family. I give you all resentment or regret I've carried toward them. (Pause and give your negative feelings to the Lord.)

And I want to honor and love my adoptive family, both parents and siblings. I ask you to forgive me for ways I've tried to punish them because I really wanted my birth family to raise me. Please forgive me for the things I've done to test their love for me.

Today, Lord, I give you the pain for every way I've felt trapped between these two families, either by their conflicts or by circumstances that affected us all. Please enable me to see the good in each family and their role in my life.

Thank you for creating me, preserving my life, and adopting me into your family. With your help, I choose to face whatever unknowns still remain. In Jesus' name, amen.

SEVEN

TRUTH AND LIES ABOUT YOU

Do not be conformed to this world, but be transformed by the renewing of your mind, that you may prove what is that good and acceptable and perfect will of God. —Romans 12:2 NKJV

ADOPTIVE MOM—JODI

The three of us in the living room, my husband sat on the couch, and my daughter and I sat beside each other in overstuffed chairs. We'd intentionally not sat across from her because we didn't want this conversation to be "us against her." We were trying to work through some relationship issues.

Suddenly, she announced, "Pop has never liked me anyway."

Shocked, we had no idea what she meant. She went on to tell us, "On the day I greeted you and Pop at the airport, I'd already met you, Mom, but I was meeting Pop for the first time. I was standing behind the rope, waiting for you to come with your bags. Then I saw you, and Pop looked at me for the first time. I could tell he was disappointed in what he saw."

Of course, nothing was further from the truth. My husband had eagerly awaited meeting her, and he embraced her in a long, loving hug as they came together. To us it was a beautiful moment; to her, it was the next step in her life of rejection.

This adopted daughter always anticipated rejection. Even the slightest correction turned into an emotional battle because she perceived it as a complete dismissal of her as a person. She was very sensitive, and it was hard to instruct her, even gently. Her defensiveness would immediately flare. She believed everyone would eventually leave her and that she had no value. She lived inside a wall she'd built to protect herself emotionally from the next disappointment. She built it as a young child, experiencing rejection and abandonment many times in her challenging life before adoption.

While my adopted children may have seemed happy and well-adjusted to those outside our home, I could see the lies they believed about themselves. I could see it in their responses, in their rebuffing of praise, in their shame about their stories. I could see it in the choices they sometimes made for themselves that continued patterns of brokenness. While it was often covered over in the day-to-day life of a family, when I spoke to them about deeper things of who they were, I could hear the lies they believed. The unworthiness they felt. They carried the weight of abandonment, grief and loss, and shame and isolation.

I came to realize that my children's identity had been formed before being adopted—or because of being adopted. Being in our family didn't magically correct the lies they believed about themselves. Because they carried the mark of losing their first family, being in our family actually helped build the narrative of these lies. They were deeply embedded in their self-worth and potential.

I wanted my love to be enough for my children. I wanted it to overcome all the lack of love they'd experienced. But my love could never be enough, because I was also a broken person who had her own issues and believed her own lies about herself. Both my children and I needed something much greater to come to a place of healing.

I had to teach my daughter who always expected rejection that it was not about her being loved by her first parents or her second parents. I had to teach her that, most importantly, it was about her being created and loved by God. And I had to believe that about myself in order to teach that to her. I had to come to understand that God is my parent, and that I have also been given the gift of adoption by being welcomed into His family. If I could truly ground my own identity as a child of God, I could also give this identity to my child.

I didn't know all these things when I began raising my children. Yes, I took them to church, but I didn't really understand how central this identity must be to their thriving. I'm seeing all this now through the rearview mirror. A child who comprehends and embraces their adoption as a redemption from God will do well in life and relationships. But a child who can't reach this synthesis of understanding can remain adrift, buffeted by the waves of life, and not stand on the solid ground of identity rooted as a child of God. This essential truth played out in our family and in our children's choices as they entered adulthood.

As a parent, I needed to make their paternity with the Creator God, manifested in Jesus Christ, the absolute central issue of raising my children. A child who's fully rooted in that identity will be more willing to trust that God has a plan for restoring their life. A child who rejects this identity will often reject the love of a second family and struggle to find wholeness. Without this identity as a child of God, the turmoil of reconciling who they are, their first family, their second family, and all the whys of their loss can torment a child and keep them reeling well into adulthood.

This is also why the teen years are so excruciatingly difficult for foster and adoptive parents. The work of adolescence is comprehending and integrating one's identity. So any unanswered questions or broken places in the child's self-concept will come bubbling up to the surface as they form and shape their identity. In our family, this is when many things unraveled and challenges mounted for some of our children.

Some adopted children are still searching for their "true" identity in adulthood and try to find it in other families, or in marriage, or in a career. In their later years, some adoptive mothers have told me that much to their heartbreak, their children still struggle in middle age.

I needed to remind my children, daily, that their identity was first and foremost as a child of God. This had to supersede lies they might be accepting from the enemy.

Now I see that I needed to remind my children, daily, that their identity was first and foremost as a child of God. This had to supersede lies they might be accepting from the enemy. With this approach, the resolution of their identity as a member of my family or their family of origin took a second place to their primary identity as a beloved child of God.

In the adoption community, people often say, "Love is not enough." We say this because, despite pouring out all our love for our children and using trauma-informed parenting and striving for attachment, our children still struggle. Yes, it's true that our love isn't enough. We are incomplete and flawed humans, and so our love is also incomplete and never "enough." But God's love is enough—and it always will be!

Looking back, I wish I had often spoken the following manifesto to my children. While I may have communicated it in bits and pieces, these words capture my heart and true wishes for each of them, regardless of how they came into our family.

Jesus is the author and finisher of your life. He has a great plan for you. I am not your savior or your redeemer. I am not the one you have to thank. God is who created you, knows your name, and knows your story from beginning to end.

If you ground your identity firmly in Him, you cannot be shaken by the tragedies that will befall you. It's not about your being in our family. You have been and will always be a child of God, first and foremost. Place your identity there, and you will be able to make sense of the rest of your story.

The decision to place your identity in Christ is a decision that only you can make. Whether you accept your identity in this family matters little compared to your identity with God. I hope and pray you will choose our family as a gift from God. But beneath that, you have to put your identity firmly in the Creator or you will be wandering through life trying to figure out who you are through an endless forest of options. Your identity lies within you as a beloved child with a purpose and a plan and a destiny. I can't create that for you, no matter how much I try to help you attach or be part of our family. You can only do this for yourself.

You have to see yourself as part of an eternal family with a Father who will never leave you or forsake you. I am a flawed individual who can't make any of it right. I can't resolve your loss, and I can't fix it. And I will continue making my own mistakes. Only God can heal. Only God can make it right. He is our redeemer. If you look at me to solve these broken hurts in your life, you will surely be disappointed. I came to this relationship with my own hurts and wounds. I can't fix mine any more than I can fix yours. But I can point you to the One who has redeemed my life and brokenness. I can share with you how knowing Jesus has changed everything for me.

It's with Jesus that I can leave my hurts and sins. It's He and He alone who can heal my heart and your heart. God's love is always enough. His love is always pure, and it's always perfect, and it's always available. He is the ultimate attachment parent! He loves you beyond your comprehension. Remember that. Stand on that.

Freedom Prayer for Adoptive Parents

Please read this entire freedom-giving prayer before praying it. Then pray the parts relevant for you, adding anything you think needs to be included and remembering to engage your heart. Also, of course, use the pronoun that fits your child.

Lord, first, thank you for adopting me into your family and for helping me teach my child that they, too, are adopted into your big and loving family. Please direct me to help them see that you, God, are their primary parent. That you are their creator, and that you know them, love them, and as they're told in Deuteronomy 31:6, will never leave them nor forsake them. I pray that their heart and mind are healed of every lie that would hold them back from the destiny you have for them.

Lord, I, too, need your healing from lies I've believed. Please forgive me for so quickly believing that I'm a failure or that I don't have what it takes to parent this child. Forgive me for agreeing with any words of rejection spoken to me by my child.

I know John 8:44 tells us Satan is the father of lies, and I want no partnership with him or his deception. As you show me each lie I've believed, I will break my agreement with it and replace it with your truth. I want my mind and heart filled with your truth.

I especially ask you to show me any lies of false responsibility. Please forgive me if I'm trying to be my child's healer or savior, or trying to make up for the love they lacked in their first family or foster families. (Pause and receive God's forgiveness.)

Lord, I choose to release myself from being my child's healer or savior, even though you know I care and will pray for them. You created my child, and you are the only one

who can bring a depth of healing to their heart. Today I
choose to release the burden of having to make up to them
for every lack from the past. (Release the lies coming out
of false responsibility.)

*Please heal me from the effects of these lies and fill me
to overflowing with your truth and fresh strength. In Jesus'
name, amen.*

BIRTH MOM—LISA

Who was I anyhow?

I was a young, pregnant teenager in foster care. I was lost and
scared. People made assumptions about me based on the little
bit they knew. I believed I was unacceptable and unloved. But if
nobody wanted me and my baby, I would take care of us myself.

I prided myself on being strong and self-sufficient. I could
handle things even if I was only in high school. I rode the city
bus to prenatal appointments, took my vitamins, signed up for
childbirth classes, and studied for my honors classes. Maybe if
I made straight As, people would think I was a person of some
worth.

Despite my efforts to appear acceptable, though, in my heart
I was terrified. I had no idea what the future held for me and my
child. I was also unworthy. I had failed in my religious upbringing and disgraced my family.

The pressure to place my baby for adoption was relentless.
I was given the assignment to draw a line vertically down the
center of a piece of paper, then write my name at the top on
one side and "adoptive parents" on the other side. Under our
names, I was instructed to make a list of what each of us could
give my child. This was a lesson in devastation—and frankly,
manipulation. Any hope I had was crushed at that moment.
I feared I would be on the streets with my newborn if I didn't

give in. I had nothing to offer my child, and I felt unworthy to be his mother.

Unacceptable. Unloved. Unworthy.

The weight of these accusations sat heavy on my chest, and there were moments when I felt I couldn't breathe. Then I met Jesus, and He changed everything. My faith was new, and my understanding of the Bible was minuscule, but something was changing. I was changing. The Holy Spirit was stirring in my heart, and I was beginning to grasp just how deep the Father's love for me was. I was learning about an enemy who sought to destroy me by dumping buckets of water on the tiny flame of my faith. He wanted me to doubt God, to think this newfound belief in a personal and real Savior was just my way of coping with fear and loss.

But I was like a small child clinging tightly to Jesus' hand. He had reached down to me, and I had put my hand in His. In my childlike faith, I was confident that if I let go, He would hold my hand even more firmly. He was going to keep me safe. Psalm 73:23–24 says, "Yet I am always with you; you hold my right hand. You guide me with your counsel" (CSB).

Everyone I loved had left me, or so it seemed at the time, and I had believed I was unlovable. I'd believed I was unacceptable to God. But He held me close to His heart. I often felt panicked and scared, but I imagined myself in His arms. I wasn't unacceptable to Him. He loved me and wasn't disappointed in me.

The night after Christopher was born, a young nurse came into my room. She saw my tears and asked if she could help. I told her about the adoption plan and that I was completely heartbroken. Her eyes reflected my sadness, and she spoke gentle words of compassion.

Then she asked, "Do you know Jesus?"

I explained that I had just committed my life to Him, but it was all brand-new. She sat on the side of my bed and began explaining the gospel. Then she read these words to me from the book of Romans: "God showed his great love for us by sending Christ to die for us while we were still sinners" (Romans 5:8 TLB). God's love for me was great, and He had sent Jesus to die for my sins. He loved me even before I knew Him. I was lovable after all—so lovable that Jesus went to the cross for me. This was truly good news.

I had a new identity—beloved daughter of my Father in heaven and friend of Jesus. I resonated with the story of the woman in the Gospel of Luke who brought a valuable jar of perfume to a house where Jesus was having dinner. She wasn't invited. She wasn't the kind of person an important religious leader would have allowed in his home. Can you imagine the courage that took? She was so desperate for Jesus and so incredibly grateful to Him that she had the courage to walk into that room.

In His presence, she knelt by Jesus, weeping, and her tears fell on His feet. She kissed His feet, then wiped them with her hair and poured the fragrant oil on them. Her heart was broken by her own sinfulness, and in His presence, all she could do was weep. She showed love and honor in the ways she knew.

The story continues:

> When the Pharisee who had invited him saw this, he said to himself, "This man, if he were a prophet, would know who and what kind of woman this is who is touching him—she's a sinner!"
>
> Jesus replied to him, "Simon, I have something to say to you."
>
> He said, "Say it, teacher."
>
> "A creditor had two debtors. One owed five hundred denarii, and the other fifty. Since they could not pay it back, he graciously forgave them both. So, which of them will love him more?"
>
> Simon answered, "I suppose the one he forgave more."
>
> "You have judged correctly," he told him. Turning to the woman, he said to Simon, "Do you see this woman? I entered your house; you gave me no water for my feet, but she, with her tears, has washed my feet and wiped them with her hair. You

gave me no kiss, but she hasn't stopped kissing my feet since I came in. You didn't anoint my head with olive oil, but she has anointed my feet with perfume. Therefore I tell you, her many sins have been forgiven; that's why she loved much. But the one who is forgiven little, loves little." Then he said to her, "Your sins are forgiven."

Those who were at the table with him began to say among themselves, "Who is this man who even forgives sins?"

And then Jesus turns to the woman—the one who's unworthy to be in that room, the one whose sins were so grievous—and says these words:

"Your faith has saved you. Go in peace."

Luke 7:39–50 CSB

This woman was my example. I was lost in my sin, scorned by people who looked at me, a young pregnant teen, with disdain. But Jesus loved me, and I had no words to express the depth of my gratitude. I wanted to weep over His feet and anoint them with perfume. His love changed everything. More than forty years later, I think of this woman and know that I, too, have been forgiven much and that I love the Lord deeply in return.

We have an enemy who seeks to destroy us. When we're experiencing deep loss, the lies he speaks in our ears seem to ring with truth.

Friend, I don't know what led you down this painful path. Maybe you made the best plan you could for your child. Or maybe your life was filled with so much turmoil and suffering that your child was removed from your care. Perhaps your parental rights were terminated. But no matter how our circumstances may differ, each one of us has believed lies about who we are.

We have an enemy who seeks to destroy us. When we're experiencing deep loss, the lies he speaks in our ears seem to ring with truth and we are even more vulnerable. When life feels hopeless and our hearts are aching, we are more open to his attacks. As we'll learn more in Part Four of this book, this is when we must cling to the truths of the Bible and pray with power.

You are forgiven. You are loved. You are held. You are not alone.

Freedom Prayer for Birth Moms

If you've already prayed this prayer in the past, ask the Holy Spirit if He would have you pray it again. If the answer is yes, then pray the parts relevant for you, adding anything you think needs to be included and remembering to engage your heart.

Lord, I want to update my repentance. Please forgive me for each and every way I sinned in connection with my becoming a birth mother. I receive your forgiveness. (Pause and really receive God's forgiveness.) *And because you've forgiven me, I choose to forgive myself for my past sin.* (Now forgive yourself.)

I ask forgiveness for believing lies about myself and letting them be the lenses through which I see myself and my life. Today I want to come out of agreement with each and every lie I've embraced, such as lies that say I'm unworthy, unloved, and unacceptable. I also come out of agreement with the lie that my life is permanently stained or ruined and that I have to accomplish something extra to pay for my failures. I'm ready to renew my mind and come into agreement with what you say about me. Please help me break the chains that these lies have put around my mind

*and heart. Thank you for showing me the truth about who
I am.*

*Holy Spirit, Teacher, please alert me any time I'm slipping
back into agreement with the old lies, and bring me back
into your truth. In Jesus' name, amen.*

ADOPTEE—BETSY

Even after I'd become an adult, in my head a voice still blasted
as though from a loudspeaker:

"You are a mistake."

"You don't belong."

"You shouldn't even be here on the earth."

"You're not worthy of love."

"If people knew the real you, they'd reject you."

"When something goes wrong, it's your fault."

The barrage of these lies continued relentlessly day and night.
They built an impenetrable fortress around my mind, keeping
me trapped.

Because of the unique wounds of adoption, adoptees are particularly vulnerable to believing lies about themselves. I was no
exception. Before family gatherings, I often thought, *I'm just a
nobody going nowhere. Why would anyone even want to include
me?* When special opportunities came my way, I often bought
into the lie that I would probably just mess up, so I shouldn't
even try. Encompassing my life, these kinds of lies were as normal to me as breakfast cereal.

The biggest problem, however, was that I didn't know I was
believing lies! After all, they seemed true. They felt true. How
shocked I would have been if I'd realized these falsehoods were
actually setting the very trajectory of my life. The thief, who
comes to "steal and kill and destroy" (John 10:10), was having
a heyday watching me stumble and bumble through life. The

father of lies had a solid grip on my mind (John 8:44). I had bought into a whole web of entrapping lies.

Some years later I discovered a saying that summed it up so well:

> If you accept a belief, you reap a thought.
> If you sow a thought, you reap an attitude.
> If you sow an attitude, you reap an action.
> If you sow an action, you reap a habit.
> If you sow a habit, you reap a character.
> If you sow a character, you reap a destiny.[1]

Now read just the first line and the last line. Can you see the powerful connection between the things you believe and your destiny? The thief works in subtle ways. He whispers super-negative thoughts into our minds, but here's the trap: we think these are our own thoughts. We have no idea we're being ruthlessly lied to. So here I was, striving to become the best version of myself I could be but simultaneously agreeing with horrendous lies.

Weary and discouraged, cowering inside my dark fortress of lies, I knew something was wrong. *But what is it? How can I fix it?* I pondered. I felt crazy, because in addition to my darkness, I also had a light side. I knew the things Jesus had said to me that Easter morning were true. For a while I could believe that I belonged to Him and that I was truly lovable. What a relief! But then, like dark storm clouds coming to overshadow a sunny day, my fragile light would be extinguished, and I would again find myself trapped in my dark fortress.

> The thief whispers super-negative thoughts into our minds, but here's the trap: we think these are our own thoughts. We have no idea we're being ruthlessly lied to.

Even in my darkest times, however, I knew Jesus was there. I continued to cry out for help, for truth, for meaning in my life. Yet dark to light, light to dark, I cycled back and forth, my life seemingly out of my control.

For me, something huge was still missing. I didn't know I needed a radical mind shift. That I needed a total transformation from my old ways of thinking. I didn't know God wanted to replace my no-good, miserable thinking with His truths about me. He wanted me to come into agreement with what He said about me and for those truths to become a solid foundation in my mind and heart. He wanted my mind full of His truths, such as before the foundation of the world He knew that I belonged to Him (Ephesians 1:4–5), that He would be a loving Father to me (Ephesians 2:4), that He would never leave me or forsake me (Hebrews 13:5), and that He had purposed my life and had fulfilling things for me to do (Ephesians 2:10).

Only after many years, a failed marriage, and myriads of missed opportunities did the Lord open my eyes to the thief's evil schemes. And in His mercy, He began to free me from them.

It happened this way. I was in my thirties and feeling pretty desperate about my life. As I was making myself read the Bible one dreary morning, a verse suddenly leapt off the page: "Do not be conformed to this world, but be transformed by the renewing of your mind" (Romans 12:2 NASB).

As I read those words, something deep inside me stirred, became unsettled. *Lord, is this where I'm stuck?* I questioned. *Is this my problem? Does my mind need an overhaul? Does it need to be transformed?*

In my spirit, I heard a very loud and resounding *Yes!*

One of the specific lies I believed was that somehow, as an adopted child, I was "less than" natural, biological children. Believing that I was "less than" could apply to any or all situations. It was like the "given," the baseline of my life. For example, I was less acceptable, less talented, less stable, less able to succeed.

Our words shape our world, and I continually sabotaged myself with my "less than" lie.

From that moment on, the Holy Spirit became my teacher, teaching me the pathway to the freedom I yearned for (John 14:26). And in the subsequent years, He taught me the following:

- Core lies within our belief system are formed in our childhoods through hurtful experiences.
- Other lies we believe come from our family, friends, and influential people in our lives.
- Lies can even become established in us while we're still in our mother's womb, especially if her life and surroundings are traumatic while she's pregnant.[2]
- The most destructive lies we believe are about ourselves. These relate to who we are—our identity. Other significant lies are about God Himself or others.
- Another category of lies appears to be true according to the "facts" of a situation, but they're not the highest level of truth according to God's Word. For example, facts say, *I have an illness.* God's truth says, *God wants to heal me.* He wants us to embrace the truth—His truth.

We frequently see three destructive patterns with orphans or those who have experienced abandonment. (I had one of them.)

Pattern A: Abandonment and resulting feelings of rejection lead to a pattern of striving to achieve and people pleasing in an effort to win love, acceptance, and worth.

Pattern B: This second pattern also begins with abandonment. But it escalates into anger, rage, and rebellion—and often into self-sabotaging behaviors such as addiction, suicide attempts, and sometimes violence.

Pattern C: This pattern issues into resignation and passivity. It leads to a wasted life.

Which pattern a person acts out is related to personality and the types of trauma experienced, but it's always a subconscious cry for help.

Each of these three patterns has places where it's easy to get stuck, hooked. Each also combines with other lies. Often, the various lies reinforce each other or create a setup where one can't win.

My pattern, pattern A, was that I could never do enough, be enough, or accomplish enough to be sure I wasn't still "less than." Working along with this basic lie was an additional lie that put me into a double bind—a no-win situation. Can you guess what the additional lie was? I simply believed that no matter how hard I tried, it wouldn't be good enough, and so I was defeated before I even started.

One day after I'd completed two master's degrees as well as a specialist degree in counseling, the Lord impressed on my heart that I was "more than enough" for Him to accept and love me without my having any degrees at all.

Wow! Really, God?

That day I replaced my "less than" lie with God's truth that I am "more than enough." Now I could rest. I had nothing further to prove. Nothing.

I knew it was time to kick all the lies I'd believed out of my life. As I broke agreement with each one, new thoughts began to come. It was as if my old fortress of lies now had two doors as the Holy Spirit began working with me to renew my mind. At one door, the old vicious lies were going out. At the other, God's new, wonderful truths were coming in.

My lies had been like an interstate highway in my mind, down which I had frequently traveled. I needed time, determination, and persistence to break up this easily traveled route and lay down a new Highway of Truth.

Have you ever had a good night's sleep after a period of sleep deprivation? You wake up feeling like a new person fully alive. That's how it was for me when I was able to say, "Yes, I do belong!" Regardless of how the egg and sperm came together that made up my life, it was God who formed me in my mother's womb. It was God who had planned my life and a fulfilling destiny for me (Jeremiah 1:5).

I was beginning to feel a sense of belonging, beginning to feel worthy of having an opinion, beginning to feel worthy going to family occasions and embracing opportunities. At last the exhausting pattern of striving to please people, to win their acceptance and love, had been broken. I moved from performance and what I could do to reconcile two sets of families to my identity with the Father—and I became an "acceptable daughter." That was when I got my purpose from God. Clear signs showed I was on God's prayerful way to freedom.

When you get to chapter 12, you'll find Going Deeper prayers to help you address lies you've believed.

Freedom Prayer for Adoptees

Please read this entire freedom-giving prayer before praying it. Then pray the parts relevant for you, adding anything you think needs to be included and remembering to engage your heart. If you're praying for a child under the age of ten or who lacks the maturity to pray with you, pray over that child while they're sleeping. This is just as effective and can be easier for both of you.

> *Lord, please forgive me for every lie I've allowed to control or influence my life and for every relationship and every*

opportunity I've sabotaged because of it. I receive your forgiveness. (Stop and focus your attention on receiving God's forgiveness.)

Lord, your Word tells me Satan is the father of lies, and I'm ready to break my agreements with him and the lies he says about me. I'm ready to get rid of the crippling patterns resulting from these lies that have been stealing the abundant life you want for me.

I especially come out of agreement with the lies that I am a mistake, that I have no value, and that I will never amount to anything. I break agreement with the lie that I have to work harder to compensate for being a "nobody."

Lord, open my eyes and expose every lie I've believed, especially lies about myself. Enable me to uproot these lies and replace them with your truth as you help me renew my mind so I'll begin to see myself as you see me. In Jesus' name, amen.

EIGHT

HURTS AND WOUNDS

The Spirit of the LORD *is upon Me, because He has anointed Me to preach the gospel to the poor; He has sent Me to heal the brokenhearted, to proclaim liberty to the captives and recovery of sight to the blind, to set at liberty those who are oppressed.* —Luke 4:18 NKJV

ADOPTIVE MOM—JODI

We were sitting together in overstuffed chairs at the local bookstore on a beautiful Saturday morning. My recently adopted teen son had a voracious love of books, and this was one way I could connect with him—encouraging his pursuit of knowledge. He was also a big fan of the bookstore's coffee, and the combination of caffeine and quiet sometimes gave him the space to open up and tell me more about himself.

So after he completed his assigned chores early as usual, we would occasionally sneak away from our hectic house on Saturday mornings while the other kids did theirs. As you can imagine, I enjoyed these special dates immensely.

I adjusted myself in the chair, sipped my latte, and peeked over my novel at my son's handsome face as he studied a book about science. He's a quiet person and a man of few words. Sitting in silence with him was not uncomfortable but wonderful. We'd learned to do it well as we spent a lot of time in his home nation during the adoption process, watching movies and taking walks and learning to be quiet with each other. Sometimes connection is talking, and sometimes it's just the gift of presence. I loved being present with this son.

As my attention drifted back to my novel, he looked up from his book and said in an even voice, "I should probably tell you about the three times I almost died."

I tried not to choke on my coffee or overreact. The thought of my son almost dying even once took my breath completely away. I adored everything about him. I set down my book, steeled my heart, and looked toward him. And then in detail he told me about three times his very short life had already been threatened by illness and injury and neglect.

It had taken him all these months to tell me. I knew the highlights of his life story—where he'd lived, how he'd survived. He'd written it all out for me in detail because I needed it for the adoption court proceedings. But those were just facts, not feelings. Those were places and names and dates. Those were not hurts and wounds. On this day, during our coffee and reading date, our relationship had reached a place of felt safety where he was ready to share the deeper hurts of his life with me. The traumas. The tragedies. I was grateful but also grieved.

When you raise a baby from birth, you know every cough, scrape, and hurt they experience. You know about the time a beloved pet died or a bully in the fourth grade made them cry. You know the tender places and the tough spots in their story. A mother knows her biological child like no one else on earth if she has the great fortune of raising that child from birth.

But for a fostered or adopted child, this deep intimacy of being completely known by a mother or father has been disrupted. Who knows them best? Who knows the times they were most deeply hurt—physically or emotionally? Who is the one person they can count on when the sorrows of life overwhelm them and a hurt from the past becomes a factor in the present? Tragically, many foster children and adoptees don't have such a person. Their life is a patchwork of caregivers and relatives and survival. Only they themselves hold the complete story of the hurts and wounds that shape their very soul.

One of my daughters has a lot of scars on her body from her hard early life. They're clearly visible, and I would ask her about them over time. It took me a while to know the story behind each of them, but I made a point to understand. At least these scars were visible, and I could ask for the story. What's taken so much longer—and is a journey we still travel together—is my knowing and understanding the scars that aren't visible. The scars from hurts and wounds in her soul.

We enter every relationship with the scars we bring. Intimacy in marriage or adult friendship means opening up, sharing our past hurts and wounds, and letting others know and understand us more deeply. A child, however, doesn't have language for this exercise. A child doesn't know how to tell you about open emotional wounds. And so as a mother, I found myself often inadvertently bumping into those wounds and triggering a trauma response from my child. Loving a child who's been hurt is loving a child with wounds, both visible and invisible.

I know how to dress a visible wound. I love the attachment-parent coaching that suggests the use of bandages for any seen or unseen hurt presented by a small child who comes into your home through foster care or adoption. We went through boxes and boxes of Spiderman and princess Band-Aids at our house. I understood the theory behind this technique and supported it. Without a mother to attend to wounds in infancy, my child needed their new mother to make up for that lack by over-compensating now. So when my child came to me with a tiny scratch or scrape, I made a big fuss. I put Band-Aids on wounds I couldn't even see. I comforted and consoled.

But that strategy didn't give me all I needed for the deeper wounds. I can't see deeper wounds, and they can't be healed by my soothing. Deeper wounds in all our souls can be healed only by the great healer, the one who made us, the Creator Himself.

I had to accept that I can't heal the deepest wounds done to my teen son. I wasn't there the days those things happened to him. I couldn't protect him, no matter how much I wished I could. I can't make up for the way those around him caused those trials or responded to them. I can't go back and rewrite that script that will always be part of his story. I can't rescue him from being in harm's way. He was.

> My children came to me with deep wounds that had nothing to do with me. All I can do is remind them that there is Someone who can take those hurts now.

What I had to face as a mother is that I can't rely on my own strength and care to heal any of that. My children came to me with hurts and deep wounds that had nothing to do with me. I wanted to know about them, and I wanted to understand how to interact with my child in a way that accounts for those tender places, but I can't take them away. All I can do is remind them that there is Someone who can take those hurts now. There's a loving God who wants to heal every open wound in their heart. There's a Father who has loved and does love them more than I ever can.

And I had to give this same advice to myself when parenting a child from a difficult background caused me to have my own hurts and wounds. The life of a foster or adoptive parent is not an easy path. We've all heard the adage "Hurting people hurt people." Foster and adoptive children are suffering from hurts and wounds, and sometimes we're the subject of that hurt being passed along to us, the new parent, the person closest to them.

Some of the deepest hurts I've experienced have come from being in a relationship with my adopted children. It's hard to write that sentence, but it's simply true. An adoptive mother opens her heart to receive a child she doesn't know and did not birth. It's a particularly vulnerable kind of heart opening, which exposes the tenderest parts of one's heart to receive this child as one's very own. It requires great courage, and as it turns out, it also comes at great cost. But I can also say that God has healed every one of those hurts. My heart today is full and tender, not scarred and closed.

My adopted children—as well as my biological daughter—are the best gifts I've received in my life, and each one is a treasure in my soul. I love my adopted children as passionately and as fiercely as I love the child I birthed. When these children, out of their own past traumas, lashed out or rejected me or chose to intentionally hurt me, it felt like the most unjust of wounds. I thought, *How can the person I've given my life for be the very one to cut me so deeply?*

This is the challenge we face as foster and adoptive parents. It's a journey that we alone understand and why we need one another so desperately. When people outside our community hear about some of the poor choices our children make or the way we're sometimes treated, it can seem shocking and even unbelievable to them. But those walking this journey will nod in recognition and solidarity. In reaching for love, we as foster and adoptive parents are often met with great rejection.

I'm still on the journey of working this out with God. I know to the very core of my being that these are the children God intended for me to parent. I know I was His choice for them as a redemption of brokenness. I believe this completely. God is sovereign, and He does not make mistakes. So I have come to accept that if He sent this challenge into my life, it was for my own sanctification. I must have needed it.

Perhaps I was looking for a reward when I adopted. Perhaps I thought of myself too highly or too nobly. Perhaps my life was far too easy and comfortable. I'm sure these and many other tendencies were true of me. But God knew what I needed. Parenting children born to another has changed me in a way nothing else has. It's changed me more than marriage, more than illness, more than the deaths of loved ones. Parenting my adopted children has stretched me, expanded me, taught me, humbled me, broken me, filled me, encouraged me, inspired me, created me. I am the me of today because of being a mother to these children. Recognizing this, I've come to accept the trials as a necessary part of a beautiful life.

I love roses, and my husband is faithful about planting and cultivating rosebushes for me. Every spring our home is filled with lovely roses he collects from our yard. He brings in the gorgeous cuttings, and my role is to trim them and place them in vases around our house. This is a tricky job. Roses have sharp thorns. When I first began decorating with them, I was often hurt by the thorns because I lacked experience in understanding the rose.

But over time, I developed a way of handling them that didn't hurt me so much. I found a way to appreciate their beauty and avoid the thorns. I love my roses, and I love the beauty they bring to my home.

I think you understand the analogy I'm making. My children are beautiful and fill my home with God's glory, His story of redemption. I accept their thorns, and I continue to ask God to help me handle them in a way that brings glory to Him.

Freedom Prayer for Adoptive Parents

Please read this entire freedom-giving prayer before praying it. Then pray the parts relevant for you, adding anything you think needs to be included and remembering to engage your heart. Also, of course, use the pronoun that fits your child.

> *Lord, I ask today for your help and your wisdom as I continue to learn about my child's deep, often invisible wounds. I need the courage to face their pain, not avoid it. Give me strength to deal with it in a godly way rather than minimizing it. Help me teach them, Lord, that you are their healer.*
>
> *I ask you to forgive me for those times I've put up walls or turned away from my child's pain because it seemed like too much to handle. Forgive me for protecting myself. Forgive me for all the times I've resented this part of my job as a parent and just wanted to resign.* (Pause and receive the Lord's forgiveness.)
>
> *Help me, Lord, to forgive my child for all the ways they've hurt me and caused my own heart to ache. Today I choose to continue forgiving them.*
>
> *Lord, I give you the pain I've experienced because of my child's pain. I also give you my own hurts and pain from their rejecting me, from the ways they've punished me, from their acting out and shaming me, and from their acts of self-sabotage.*
>
> *Also, if I've become emotionally numb, I ask you to heal my heart so I can feel again. Please empower me to continue to choose to be my child's parent.* (Pause and name every pain and negative feeling. Then release them to the Lord. If you're a visual person, "see" yourself giving your pain to Jesus or placing it at the foot of His cross.)
>
> *Thank you for being a God of new beginnings and for filling me with courage and wisdom so that both my child*

and I receive the depth of the healing you have for each of us. In Jesus' name, amen.

BIRTH MOM—LISA

It was Mother's Day, and I was sitting with the teens in a pew near the front of the church. Most kids sat with their families, but we high schoolers sat in a group. I'd moved back home with my parents six months after my son was born. During my year in foster care, I lived with strangers in a city, attended a large high school, and gave birth to my sweet baby. I also came to know Jesus. I was not the same person, and everything felt different.

The small, white church on the corner welcomed me, and the youth group embraced me. But today I felt alone in their midst. This was the day I'd been dreading. I had a son, and I loved him with all my heart. But was I a mother?

The pastor preached a sermon about mothers, and then two women walked to the front with baskets of pink carnations. They moved down the aisles handing flowers to each mom as they passed. My heart was pounding, and I thought I might burst into tears as they passed me by.

Then we rose to sing, and I felt someone touch my arm. I turned to see a woman with a kind smile offering me a flower. Grateful tears ran down my cheeks. In nearly every part of my life, I had to pretend I was a normal teenager. But here, in this church that had taken me in when my heart was shattered, I wasn't judged but known.

I met my husband, Russ, at that little white church during our senior year of high school. We went to college together and got married after our junior year, moving into family housing on campus. We'd been married a little more than two years when I got pregnant with our first child. Now, finally, I could be a mother, and this wound would begin to heal.

I had no idea how many times friendly, well-meaning people would ask, "Is this your first?" When it came to medical providers, it was a given that I would tell them about Christopher, but I struggled with nearly everyone else. Russ and I had settled in Seattle after graduation, where he continued his studies. No longer in a small town where everybody knew my story, I could blend in like any other pregnant woman. Each time I was asked this question, I faced the dilemma of deciding how to answer. Most commonly I replied, "Yes, this is our first baby."

Our daughter was born early on a brisk March morning in our apartment near Pike Place Market. Two wise and experienced midwives were with us. The idea of birthing my baby in a hospital, a place where I'd experienced such severe trauma, was unthinkable to me. I would labor at home where I felt safe and nobody could take my baby from my arms.

Years passed, and the Lord gave me more children. Being a mom gave me joy, and I took great delight in my kids. But the wound of losing my first child didn't disappear. I carried the loss with me through my days, and I prayed for him.

Not until years later did I know he also experienced a wound that didn't spontaneously heal. He had parents who loved him, a sister, and a big extended family, but he thought of me. He wondered about his story and wanted to know if I loved him. He felt a strange attachment to this mother he couldn't remember but still knew. He began searching for me when he was sixteen.

> Adoption was the solution for my unplanned pregnancy, but we both knew we'd lost someone. We both felt sorrow and shame. He felt rejected. I felt unworthy.

I once heard an adoptive father and pastor say, "Adoption is so beautiful." I replied, "I guess it depends if you're on the giving or receiving end." Adoption was the solution for my unplanned pregnancy, but our separation left me and my son with deep wounds. We both knew we'd lost someone. In the absence of any information, we both felt sorrow and shame. He felt rejected. I felt unworthy.

We carried our questions separately, and later, after we re-united, we talked through them together. When we saw each other after being separated for many years, there was a deep sense of peace, like a long exhale. Being together, face-to-face, eased some of the past, but it didn't replace the missing years.

My healing came in the presence of the Lord and in the deep, secure love of my husband, Russ. My son, whom I'd named Christopher but whose parents named him Nick, struggled with many challenges. But in time, Nick found comfort in the hard work of recovery and finding God in his community there. Some of our hurts and wounds may disappear. Mine became faded scars that remind me of the grace and kindness of God who continues to heal and restore my heart.

Freedom Prayer for Birth Parents

Please read this entire freedom-giving prayer before praying it. Then pray the parts relevant for you, adding anything you think needs to be included and remembering to engage your heart. Also, of course, use the pronoun that fits your child.

> Lord, in Luke 4:18 we see that you said you came to heal the brokenhearted and bind up their wounds. But how can you bind wounds from a distance? Draw close to me, Lord. Let me sense your presence. Let me sense your love. Pour your words of life and hope into my heart where it's been shattered. Please put it back together again as only you can.
>
> Today I forgive all those who failed me and made my situation even more painful. (Pause and forgive those who

come to mind.) *I also continue to forgive my child's adoptive parents for any way they've failed my expectations of raising them.*

Lord, I release to you the intense feelings of loneliness I experienced when I released my child for adoption and the sense that no one really understood how fragile and grieved I was. I give you the agonizing feelings of having to pretend that nothing had happened. I give you the sadness and sorrow of the "missing years" with my child. Please take it all. I can no longer carry it. (Pause and name every pain and negative feeling. Then release them to the Lord. If you're a visual person, "see" yourself giving your pain to Jesus or placing it at the foot of His cross.)

With your help, I choose to lay down all the ways I've used to escape from my pain. I choose to begin to receive your healing today. Fill my heart afresh with your love. In Jesus' name, amen.

ADOPTEE—BETSY

Your story can be healed. Your child's story can be healed. That's the good news! I know it. I've experienced it in my own life, and I've seen this happen in hundreds of other lives.

We three authors have been transparently describing our own places of personal struggles around adoption. These include the loss Lisa experienced in placing her baby for adoption, the challenge Jodi faced as she realized her love alone wasn't enough to bring the needed healing to her adopted children's issues, and the turmoil I experienced as I tried to find my place of belonging, value, and identity.

While every person has their own unique story related to adoption, we also share many commonalities. Many of us feel loss, grief, shame, fear, and inward turmoil. What we may not realize, however, is that God is just waiting to enter our stories in a powerful way, a way that brings fresh hope and healing. Have you invited Him into your story?

My first and perhaps most significant healing experience was totally unexpected. I didn't know God healed people's hearts today.

It happened this way. Jacque, a faithful friend, was visiting that evening. We were talking and sipping peppermint tea.

"Betsy," she said as the evening progressed, "I believe we should pray. I have a real sense that Jesus wants to touch something in your life." Neither of us knew what it might be. But a few moments later, Jacque continued. "Just bow your head and ask Jesus to come and heal you."

I had never done anything like this before, yet I trusted Jacque enough to follow her suggestion. Bowing my head, in my mind's eye I began to see a tiny baby girl who'd just been born. This baby was a deep rosy pink, and she was waving her little arms in the air. It was a lot like watching a movie. I was an observer, watching scene by scene as the story unfolded.

Suddenly, I knew the baby girl was me! Filled with amazement, I watched as a man came into the room. I immediately recognized Jesus. He picked me up, looking at me with great delight. The tender expression on His face and the beam in His eyes were like that of a proud papa who was absolutely thrilled.

"I'm so glad you're here," He said adoringly. "I love you dearly. I planned for your life a long time ago." He paused. "I won't tell you yet about everything I have for you to do, but you're going to love it. I have chosen you, and I have chosen you to do something special for me. You are going to be so fulfilled."

Then He patted me, snuggling me against His shoulder. He was loving me so tenderly, as if I were the only baby in the entire world.

Something deep inside of me broke, and hot tears slipped down my face, pouring out years of "not belonging," of feeling like an outsider. My body heaved and ached. I was sobbing and almost gasping for breath. I couldn't stop. I didn't want to stop. It felt like poison was flowing, flowing, flowing out of me for good. Time seemed to stand still during my uncontrollable upheaval. I didn't care if Jacque was there or if I looked like a wreck.

Finally, my cascade of tears subsided. I felt clean, clean to the core. It was as if Jesus, my divine physician, had gone into the core of my being and cut out the cancer made up of my pain and lies. It was gone from my life for good.

The scene began to fade. I came back to the present, to my living room, and to my friend Jacque.[1] I knew what I had seen was real. I knew I had not made it up. It was as real as the physical healing I'd once experienced from pneumonia. The Lord's word struck a powerful blow to the lies I'd believed. I now saw that He'd planned for me. He'd intended for my life to have purpose and meaning. He gave me my right to exist. My life was a gift from Him. And I'd heard these words out of His own mouth.

Just as finding the precise thread is the key to unraveling the hem of a garment, so God's revelation to me put into my hands the thread to unraveling these old lies, and powerfully, He poured healing oil into my deep wounds of abandonment and shame.

It was like a new beginning, a transformation. Like being born again—again! I knew my life had made a huge shift. Hope flooded my heart. Jesus did come to heal the brokenhearted, and that included me!

That day, little did I know I would have many experiences of healing. As Jesus spoke His words of truth, His perspective on my life, the wounds of my heart continued to be healed. As I reread the Gospels, over and over I saw where Jesus spoke healing words that brought life changes to those around Him.

For example, after Peter betrayed Him, Jesus asked Peter to feed His sheep and lambs. In doing so He reinstated Peter as one of His trusted ones. He spoke challenging but life-giving words to the Samaritan woman at the well (John 4:7–26). Think, too, of the woman who was about to be stoned because she'd been caught in adultery. Jesus said to her, "Go your way, and from now on do not sin again" (John 8:11 NRSV). Each person heard His words of life, of healing and restoration, just as I did that amazing day.

> We have a God who is alive and well and wants us whole. He still heals today if we open our hearts to Him.

Although this was new to me, I saw it in Scripture. I also saw that this was similar to when a verse of the Bible leaps into your heart while you're reading it, and you just know it's for you here and now. His words bring life.

Something powerful and new was born in my heart that day. While I knew I needed more, I'd experienced God's goodness, His compassion in a life-changing way. I had to let others know they could receive His healing too.

Jesus said He came to heal the brokenhearted (Luke 4:18). A major part of His purpose on earth was to show us His healing, to show us that we have a God who is alive and well and wants us whole. He still heals today if we open our hearts to Him.

Freedom Prayer for Adoptees

Please read this entire freedom-giving prayer before praying it. Then pray the parts relevant for you, adding anything you think needs to be included and remembering to engage your heart. If you're praying for a child under the age of ten or who lacks the maturity to pray with you, pray over that child while they're sleeping. This is just as effective and can be easier for both of you.

Lord, you said you came to heal the brokenhearted. Only you can heal the depth of the pain in my wounded heart, and I ask you to begin to heal my heart today.

Help me forgive my birth parents for not choosing to keep me, whatever their reason. Help me forgive anyone involved with my adoption to whom I've held resentment. (Pause and forgive those who come to mind.)

Isaiah 53:4 said you would carry my grief and my sorrow. Today I choose to give you every pain and negative feeling I've stored up over the years. I give you the abandonment, the anger, the sense of not belonging, and the feeling of being a second-class citizen. (Pause and name every pain and negative feeling. Then release them to the Lord. If you're a visual person, "see" yourself giving your pain to Jesus or placing it at the foot of His cross.)

Lord, I want and need a new beginning. Fill me with new life and let me see myself as you see me. In Jesus' name, amen.

NINE

DEFEATING THE ENEMY

Look, I have given you the authority . . . over all the power of the enemy; nothing at all will harm you. —Luke 10:19 CSB

ADOPTIVE MOM—JODI

A fluorescent light hummed overhead as we sat on metal chairs in the dingy Visitors Room. My beloved child had reached a point of desperation that required in-patient psychiatric hospitalization. Connections to biological family members unearthed new details from his story, details that filled holes in his memory and brought into view the true horrors of his early childhood. Events he felt might have been childhood dreams were revealed to be actual experiences, and the weight of it was crushing him.

He looked at me and said the hardest words I've ever heard as a mother: "I feel like Satan was standing there waiting for me the moment I was born."

My child knew the Bible and had actually read quite a lot of it. He had a particular fascination with good and evil from a very young age. He knew who Jesus is, and he also knew he had an enemy named Satan, hater of all that is good and true and who battles against us.

And my son felt that this enemy was waiting for him the moment he was born. How could I argue? Everything about his story felt tragic. Our attempts to find the truth, to refute rumors of terrible acts, only led to family members confirming that these rumors were true. My son's own memories told a tale of misfortune and horror that was hard to even comprehend. There was no silver lining in this story. It was agony and evil and deprivation. And it all happened to him.

If I had not known Jesus at that moment, sitting there facing my weeping child, I might have been crushed by the sorrow of it all. The place we were sitting felt devoid of hope. Yet I did know Jesus, and I know the story the Bible tells is one of His being the victor over the powers of darkness. The Bible says Jesus crushed the head of the enemy under His feet (Genesis 3:15). Jesus is often compared in Scripture to light (John 8:12). Jesus was bringing things to light, because He was the one who could overcome the darkness. Jesus was shining light in my son's dark memories so He could show His power over them in my child's life.

Nothing has brought me closer to the spiritual battle between good and evil than my journey as an adoptive mother. While we all face many trials in life, most of us consider them to be bad luck or happenstance. We tend to shy away from thinking there's an enemy who wants to thwart us and cause us harm. But if we believe in Scripture, we have to accept that this is true. Scripture clearly says we are in a battle on this side of heaven.

When you bring a broken story into your home, you also bring the full weight of the battle for redemption of that story. Are you wondering how you can defeat the enemy in your life and your children's lives? We cannot use only the solutions of this world. If the enemy is a spiritual being, he must be defeated in the spiritual. We have to fight in the spiritual—in the power of prayer. This enemy cannot be defeated any other way.

I am a doer, a fixer, a mother of action. I always want to find the solution, the fix. So it was easy to fall into the belief that to heal my child's broken heart, I just had to find the right doctor or pill or therapist. These approaches can be helpful and worthy, but as my son so poignantly stated, if the problem is spiritual, it needs a spiritual solution.

> **We have to fight in the spiritual—in the power of prayer. This enemy cannot be defeated any other way.**

As my children's spiritual covering, I must commit them to prayer. I must pray to Jesus, the victor, the lover of their lives. I must declare victory for my children's healing even before I can see it before my eyes. I have to believe they're capable of being fully healed by God, who brings the deepest kind of healing. God can touch the places in my children's hearts that man cannot reach. God can look into my children's souls and see their deepest place of emotional need. God can surround them with goodness and mercy and grace. God can make a way where there is no way.

When I had exhausted all the things I knew to do as a "fixer" mother, I realized the only one who could take this son's pain and redeem his life was Satan's defeater. So I began warring for my child in the supernatural. And I called upon many others to pray for him as well. I used every opportunity to place him at the feet of God.

And over and over again, as my son was brought through the valleys of tears and protected from his own self-destructive behaviors, I saw that God was there. He seemed to be stepping in and rescuing my son over and over, each time lifting him just a little higher. While the road was long and full of many holes, still we kept walking forward together. I felt the presence of God protecting us.

God knows every moment of my son's life. He's seen it all from beginning to end. My son can turn to Jesus, and using the very words of Christ, he can say as Jesus did, "Get behind me, Satan!" (Matthew 16:23). My son knows Jesus, and Jesus is the one writing his story. In this, my son has the power to find his way to the Light!

Recently, I texted him a video message about being called to a greater purpose (2 Corinthians 3:6). I told him, "You are called to be qualified." To my joy and surprise, he answered, "I am aware, thanks!" My son knows he's called by the Father and *will be* competent and sufficient for His purposes. The consistent prayers of many who love him and the power of our loving God have carried him through.

Your Freedom Prayer is at the end of this chapter.

BIRTH MOM—LISA

I have been walking with Jesus for more than four decades now, and my life is firmly rooted in my faith. My husband, Russ, and I have attended a wide variety of churches representing many expressions of Christian faith. Regardless of where we worshipped, though, I've always known we have an enemy who wants to turn our hearts away from God and destroy us—the Bible is clear about that. Like the three of us writing this book, you come from your own faith tradition. We invite you to join us as we strive to understand the incredible power of prayer to heal and restore.

Two decades ago, I was very sick, and we weren't sure I would recover. For the past twenty years, I'd had an autoimmune disorder. Now it was destroying all my platelets, and treatments that had worked in the past were failing. I went to bed each night afraid to fall asleep because I might have a stroke and not wake up in the morning or wake up completely changed. With seven children including a nursing baby, I feared I wouldn't see them grow up.

Through desperate tears, I told Russ I wanted our charismatic friends to gather around me, anoint me with oil, lay their hands on me, and call upon the Lord in the power of the Spirit. I was desperate for the Holy Spirit to move in my body and heal me, and I believed He could.

The Lord beautifully answered our prayers—not by physically gathering those people around me but by moving in the heart of a friend I hadn't seen in years. Michele was an oncology nurse, and the doctors she worked with were using a new treatment for patients like me. She heard how sick I was and reached out to me with this information, which I shared with my doctors. As a result, I received infusions that put me into remission for the first time in all those years, a remission that continues to this day. The Holy Spirit worked in powerful ways to answer our prayers and bring me to a place of healing.

> The Holy Spirit worked in powerful ways to answer our prayers and bring me to a place of healing.

I share this story because the teaching in this book may be unfamiliar or even make you uncomfortable. Like me all those years ago, when we thought I might die, you may be desperate for healing in your life and family. As Nick's first mom, after we were reunited, I watched him struggle with challenges while he grew up on the opposite side of the country. I prayed for him with all my heart, and I wish I'd known more powerful ways to pray.

Being an adoptive mom has driven me to my knees, crying out to God to heal my children and family. The cruelty of their early lives and the trauma they experienced have marked all of us. I want to pray with more power and more hope. I want my family to be free of the cords that entangle us. I am waging war against the enemy of our souls, who wants to destroy us.

I claim the words of the apostle Paul, who wrote, "We are hard pressed on every side, but not crushed; perplexed, but not in despair; persecuted, but not abandoned; struck down, but not destroyed" (2 Corinthians 4:8–9).

Lean into these teachings, and let's learn together.

Your Freedom Prayer is at the end of this chapter.

ADOPTEE—BETSY

If you had talked to me about "defeating the enemy" during the first forty years of my life, I would have thought you were a spiritual nut—or at least an extremist. In my mind, I'd taken everything the Bible said about the enemy and translated it into my own terms. My translation presumed that people in Bible times were actually pretty ignorant. *Poor people,* I thought. *They just labeled all the things they didn't understand as the activities of the enemy.* Looking back, I'm embarrassed to admit that I had such a superior and mocking attitude.

The more important truth, however, is that we as Christians have victory over him. God's Word tells us that "the one who is in you [Jesus] is greater [more powerful] than the one who is in the world [the enemy]" (1 John 4:4). That simply means we're already stronger than he is. Because Jesus lives inside us, we have the power to defeat him—kick him out of our lives. Why should we fear someone lesser and weaker than ourselves?

Reflecting back through the years, I remember hearing sayings such as "If you leave the enemy alone, he will leave you alone." Although this statement is a big fat lie, I bought into it. *Great,* I thought. *That settles that. I'll leave the enemy alone and be just fine.*

Unfortunately, the enemy never upholds his end of this bargain. Never once did it occur to me that he was constantly doing his work of stealing, killing, and destroying in my life

(John 10:10). For example, he continued to reinforce all the lies I'd believed about abandonment. I didn't see it, even though the Bible calls him the father of lies (John 8:44). I was also totally blinded to the fact that this same enemy might have anything to do with my paralyzing fear of death that caused me to still sleep with a light on as an adult. Furthermore, I had no clue that this enemy was putting pressure on me to repeat many of the negative generational family patterns in my family line.

> **I had no clue that this enemy was putting pressure on me to repeat many of the negative generational family patterns in my family line.**

Even though I fervently loved God and wanted to be obedient to Him, I chose to deny that the enemy, the one the Bible so often speaks of, could be impacting my life even in a small way.

Our merciful God was about to help me change my mind!

Feeling God's call in the spring of 1984, my husband and I threw our well-ordered lives into a tailspin. We packed up the best of our furniture and household goods, our clothes, and my paralyzing fear of death, and moved to a new city to attend Bible college. With all our hearts we wanted to know God and His Word more deeply and to follow Him wherever that might lead.

We got our little rental house set up, and at last it was time to begin the fall semester. With great anticipation, I found my way to the registration line. The registrar helped me sign up for my classes, but then came the unexpected. She looked straight into my eyes and said, "By the way, if you ever want to get rid of the spirit of the fear of death that's tormented you all your life, I'll be glad to help you."

I was stunned, shaking all over, and immediately engulfed in shame. Everyone in the line behind me had heard what she said. I thought, *Now they all know I'm a loser, defeated by my fear of death*. With a feeling of panic, I fled from the building, totally humiliated. In my state of brokenness, I heard an invitation to freedom as an accusation of my failure as a Christian.

Driving home, I thought about all the years I would wake up at the softest sounds, drenched in sweat because of paralyzing fear. Screaming in my mind was the tormenting thought, *Tonight I'm going to die*. I thought of the myriad times my adoptive parents had tried to reassure me I was safe. I thought about all the things I'd done to try to get free. I had fasted, and I had prayed. I had memorized Scripture about God's peace replacing fear. But nothing had worked!

Arriving home, I dumped my anger and humiliation on my husband. "How dare the registrar insult me in front of everybody? What was she thinking?"

Seeing it totally differently, he said, "Well, let's go get help! She sure saw what's been tormenting you." (Do you think he might have been tired of sleeping with a light on?)

It took several days to shift from being stuck to considering the invitation the registrar had offered. Fearfully I wondered, *But what if her help fails?*

A week later, after much prayer, my husband and I showed up at the registrar's house. During that week I'd discovered this lady had an outstanding reputation for defeating the enemy through commanding prayer. She and her team listened briefly to my story. At the same time they were apparently also listening to the Lord. As they prayed, I could feel the enemy stirring in the pit of my stomach. Then I heard a voice inside my head say, "I'm going to kill you. I'm going to choke you to death." I started coughing hard and choking for several moments. I truly felt as if I were going to die.

"Fear of death, we have authority over you. Leave now in the name of Jesus," the ministers commanded. The spirit of the fear of death began to rise up inside me. It was like a black figure. But then as I continued to cough, I felt it leave. Gone.

Quietness. Peace. After all those years of my tremendous torment, we had at last learned how to defeat the enemy. That wretched thing that had such a stranglehold on my life was actually gone.

After a genuine thank-you and drive home, my husband and I got ready for bed. Then another huge event happened. I turned out the light! Was I really lying there in the dark and feeling total peace? Yes! I could no longer remember a time when I hadn't depended on that light to protect me. It was so strange to experience peaceful darkness. It was a first, a shift, a new beginning. And my husband, patient and supportive through so many years, got to enjoy the peaceful darkness as well.

Our prayers were simple that night. "Thank you, Lord," we both murmured contentedly. "Thank you for this victory."

At last I was able to fully embrace Proverbs 3:24: "When you lie down, you will not be afraid; when you lie down, your sleep will be sweet." That night I traded all my mental health theories for a new reality: the enemy of our souls is a real enemy. Now I knew from firsthand experience that when we command him to leave in the powerful name of Jesus, he has to go. He is defeated. We have the victory.

Reflecting back with what I know now, I wonder if my fear of death came in at the time I was almost aborted. Dear reader, can you also see that as a possibility?

After having such a radical experience, which was totally out of my religious tradition, I began to study the Scriptures with a fresh openness. I found many descriptions of Jesus, as well as of His disciples, defeating the enemy and setting people free of various kinds of oppression. I also saw that as His sons and daughters, we are encouraged to follow His example.

Personally, I'm not focused on the enemy's works. On the other hand, I don't want to ignore him if I or those I love are suffering from oppression.[1]

One great piece of news is that as Christians, we can never be possessed by the enemy because possession implies ownership. Christians are owned by the Lord Jesus Christ. While Christians can be mildly to severely oppressed, we can never be owned by the enemy.

Blessings as you walk in the authority God has given you.

Chapter 12 has a Going Deeper prayer for defeating the enemy.

Freedom Prayer for All

Please read this entire freedom-giving prayer before praying it. Then pray the parts relevant for you, adding anything you think needs to be included and remembering to engage your heart.

> *Lord, thank you for beginning to reveal to me that I have a real enemy. I'm beginning to see that he may be affecting my life and/or my child's life. Your Scripture clearly warns me to not be taken advantage of by Satan because, as 2 Corinthians 2:11 says, I am "ignorant of his schemes."[2] I want to better understand how this could be happening.*
>
> *Thank you for not leaving me defenseless but giving me authority over my enemy and all his workers in the kingdom of darkness. And please forgive me for forming my beliefs about the enemy from movies I've seen or books I've read rather than from what the Bible says about him. Please help me realize that John 10:10 is true, that the enemy does actually exist and that he does come to kill, steal, and destroy.*
>
> *Lord, forgive me for ways I've ignored, denied, or mocked the enemy's existence. I also want to ask your forgiveness if I or my child needed freedom from the enemy's oppression but I didn't recognize it. (Pause and truly receive the*

Lord's forgiveness. Then based on His forgiveness, forgive yourself.)

And now I want to forgive anyone who has misinterpreted your Scripture in this area and/or caused me to fear my enemy rather than commanding him out of my life or my child's life. (Take time for the Holy Spirit to remind you of people or organizations He wants you to forgive.)

Lord, in John 8:32, your Word says, "You will know the truth, and the truth will set you free."[3] *I want to know your truth about this important area. Please lead and guide me with your fresh revelation. In Jesus' name, amen.*

TEN

FORGIVENESS

If you forgive other people when they sin against you, your heavenly Father will also forgive you. —*Matthew 6:14*

ADOPTIVE MOM—JODI

I struggle with forgiveness—deeply. I always have. I love to hold a grudge. When someone hurts me, holding that grudge feels like power. Over the course of my young life, I felt hurt by so many people and institutions. Hurt from my family of birth, hurt from my religion of birth, hurt from people who were unkind or even destructive to me. I had hurt even from being female and the injustices I experienced. I survived a sexual assault, a sex abuse scandal in my church, a deeply troubled marriage. And I had stored up a whole giant mountain of unforgiveness.

This unforgiveness weighed me down and hardened my heart. It drove me away from God and away from my family and away from the church. All I wanted to do was run. It's amazing how long you can run when the fire of unforgiveness is fueling you. In my case, it lasted not days or years but decades.

Then one day in the middle of my life, I was in a church service where the opportunity to come to the altar for prayer to release burdens was presented. At this point, I had remarried and been given a new start. But I knew I carried that burden of unforgiveness right into the marriage with me. I was already becoming adept at storing up unforgiveness for my new, devoted husband. I was desperate for a fresh perspective. I didn't want this weight in my life anymore.

As I approached the altar, the church's lead prayer minister called me to her. She said she could see that my heart had been broken and that God wanted to heal me. She laid her hand above my heart and prayed for me in the power of God. I don't remember anything else she said, but I felt my heart turn from stone to softness. I forgave. It was a supernatural experience I will never forget. That prayer restored my heart and showed me that God could mend my hurt and allow me the freedom of forgiveness. I walked back to my seat a different person—lighter, freer, full of joy.

What I didn't know then was that at that moment, God was preparing me for the greatest adventure of my life—the adventure of adopting older children from another country and culture. This journey more deeply into adoption would require me to have deep wells of forgiveness for so many relationships, including my relationship with myself.

As an adoptive mother, I faced the challenge of hearing the truth about the wounds inflicted on my children that led to their adoption. Some of these were outside the control of their biological families, such as the monster of poverty or the beast of oppression. Some of these wounds came through wickedness, like witchcraft and greed and strife. Some of these wounds were direct abuse, outside my comprehension of how one might treat a child.

Facing my children's stories required me to climb a mountain of forgiveness to be released from the unforgiveness I was carrying. So many injustices to overcome. So many people to forgive. People I hadn't even met and didn't want to know. It seemed overwhelming. But I'd learned enough about forgiveness by this season of my life to know I couldn't carry the weight of not forgiving or it would crush me.

As an adoptive mother, I also had to forgive my broken and hurting children as a daily exercise. Their rejection and poor choices trampled my heart and lured me toward the trap of resentment. I had to rise above the way they treated me and accept that their actions were born out of their own issues and not personal to me. But this was truly difficult, to say the least.

Facing my children's stories required facing a mountain of forgiveness. As an adoptive mother, I also had to forgive my broken and hurting children as a daily exercise.

I also had to forgive myself. A lot. I made so many mistakes with my children, and I probably still do. I'm still a work in progress, and I think I will be until the day Jesus takes me to heaven. I am a person who demands a lot of grace (just ask my husband). The Bible says that when we die, we will face an accounting of all our actions in life. I shudder to think of this moment. Fortunately, I've become well acquainted with forgiveness and grace by reading the Scriptures, and I cling to the hope of God's grace for me.

Everything I know and understand about forgiveness, I learned by reading the Bible. When I was young, I thought the Bible was a book full of stories about saintly people who led perfect lives and were somehow more connected to God than a person like me could be. When I began reading the Bible for myself in adulthood, I was completely shocked to learn that it's full of accounts of people who were sinful, confused, idiotic, and sometimes even wicked—just like me! These were the people God chose to do His work? Wow, I sure had it all wrong.

The Bible showed me that God chooses people for His purposes based on their heart for Him, not their perfection. He can do this because He's the source of an endless stream of forgiveness He pours out over our lives. The whole story of Jesus is a story about being forgiven. While He was walking this earth, Jesus forgave people everywhere He went. People flocked to Him to feel this cleansing bath of forgiveness. I knew if I loved Jesus, I had to show the same forgiveness He'd shown me. Jesus forgave me not just when He died on the cross for my sins, but over and over again as I seemed to fail daily as an adoptive mother. Through my devotion to Jesus, I tapped into this wellspring of forgiveness.

One of my children came into our family with so much brokenness that she didn't speak to me for almost a year. To say our relationship was challenged would be a comedic understatement. Her rejection of me cut me to the core. Yet I loved her fiercely and found myself absent of any grudge toward her. There was no explanation for my love toward her. It had to be supernatural. It had to be Jesus.

My younger self would never have had the courage or the desire to keep loving someone who was so unkind to me. But I found myself overcome with love for her, a supply that didn't run dry. I knew this couldn't be out of my own stores. I knew the level of unforgiveness I was capable of. Yet my forgiveness for her overflowed.

One day, her sister asked me, "Mom, how can you keep being so nice to her with the way she treats you?" And I gave her my honest answer. It wasn't me. I wasn't able to do it. It was Christ through me loving her. I had committed to be a vessel of His love for these children, and His powerful love was flowing through me.

Your Freedom Prayer is at the end of this chapter.

BIRTH MOM—LISA

I was cooking dinner when my phone rang. Glancing at the screen, I stopped to answer. It was my foster mom with whom I've remained friends for decades.

She asked about Nick, and as we sometimes do, we talked about the time of his birth. We wondered about the social worker, Esther, who handled his case, leading to speculation about how old she might be now. I went to my computer and searched for her name. In a flash, a photo of her as a young woman was on my screen. It was in her obituary.

As a teen, I'd viewed this woman as my enemy. Esther had taken my child and given him to somebody she deemed more worthy and acceptable. But I was one of her great failures. She could never fathom why I couldn't get on with my life. Did I really have to keep sending letters to be kept in my son's file? Did I have to keep asking if they'd heard from his adoptive family? Couldn't I just get over it like a good girl?

I harbored anger toward her because she didn't seem to grasp the sorrow that losing my son had brought to my life. Yes, she was just doing her job. And I was just one more young woman in her caseload. But I found myself asking if I could forgive someone who never acknowledged she'd hurt me.

Adoption was not beautiful to me—it represented manipulation, lies, and ultimately the sense that my child was stolen from me. This was not a willingly made adoption plan. It was defeat on a primal level. I could not speak the word *adoption* aloud. It was so charged with pain that the very thought of it overwhelmed me. Thorns of bitterness accompanied the word, forming a thick barrier.

When I married Russ, his love brought healing to my soul. Together we created a large family, with children filling my arms and easing the pain of the scar on my broken heart. The wound was still there, but it was no longer gaping except for days when a word or memory pulled away the scab.

Then sixteen years after Nick was born, he sent me an email with this subject line: "Is this for real? I'm your son."

Our reunion blew my heart wide open. Over many years, we navigated the complex relationship of family/stranger/mother and son. We developed a sweet relationship I cherish. Together we learned of lies the agency had told me and his parents. Information had been withheld that would have helped Nick. The letters I'd written for years and the St. Christopher medal I'd worn and asked the agency to keep for my son had all disappeared.

Bitterness toward the agency, my caseworker, and adoption grew until the day I realized it was consuming my thoughts and distracting me from the beauty of my life.

My bitterness toward the agency, my caseworker, and adoption grew until the day I realized it was consuming my thoughts and distracting me from the beauty of my life. Jesus had forgiven me for the many ways I'd harmed others. It was time for me to follow the lead of the apostle Paul, who wrote to the church at Ephesus, "Be kind and compassionate to one another, forgiving one another, just as God also forgave you in Christ" (Ephesians 4:32 CSB).

I knew I needed to be set free, but whom did I need to forgive? The list seemed unending: myself, my boyfriend, my parents, my caseworker, the agency. Yet forgiveness gave me compassion, and I could see everyone more clearly. We were all acting according to what we believed to be right. My parents were doing what they thought was best for me. My boyfriend was only a teenager and had little support of his own. My caseworker and agency were immersed in the societal belief that adoption was always better for children than being raised by a young, single mother.

Forgiveness brought freedom and healing to my heart. The enemy could no longer use bitterness and unforgiveness as weapons to steal my joy. The space in my mind once filled with angry thoughts was now clear and free. I had more room to consider the sweet gifts of my life and increase my capacity to minister to others.

Your story may be dramatically different. Maybe you chose your child's parents and have a beautiful, open relationship with them. You love one another as family. I hope that's your story! But separating a mother and child can happen in extreme circumstances, and somebody may have hurt you, abandoned you, or led you to believe your heart could survive this loss without help. If you've been carrying unforgiveness in your heart, do you want to be set free? Whom do you need to forgive?

That day on the phone with my foster mom, I looked at the photo of my social worker, a young woman dressed in a pink suit, a flower pinned on its lapel. Esther didn't understand me, and her beliefs blinded her to my loss, but she was not my enemy. She was simply acting according to what she believed at the time. I'd like to think I opened her eyes just a little bit and maybe changed the way she treated other young women.

Reading the obituary written by her daughter, my heart softened even more. She was a real person with a family who loved her. I closed my laptop and whispered, "I forgive you, Esther. I forgive you."

Your Freedom Prayer is at the end of this chapter.

ADOPTEE—BETSY

I have a love-hate relationship with forgiveness. I hate it because it can be so gut-wrenchingly hard. I love it because it brings relief. It clears the slate. It can reposition me from a place of revenge or retaliation to a place of peace and alignment with

God's Word. In forgiveness, I choose to take myself off the judge's seat, remove my black robes, lay down my gavel, and essentially say, *Lord, I turn this person and the job of judging them over to you.* It's a big step!

Forgiveness may be the most challenging, most daunting thing a Christian is asked to do. Forgiveness runs counter to everything in us. "It's not fair!" we cry. "They almost destroyed my life." Jesus, however, said if you have "ought" against anyone, you need to forgive (Mark 11:25–26 KJV). I certainly lived with plenty of deep "oughts," against plenty of "anyones," and my flesh delighted in schemes of retaliation. How could I forgive?

Choosing forgiveness can be considered giving a gift, an undeserved gift to the one who wounded us. Forgiveness is a choice, a gift, and undeserved. One might say, as John and Carol Arnott explain in their book *Grace and Forgiveness*, "I give you the gift of my forgiveness."[1]

We as Christians can embrace the process of forgiving others with a little more ease knowing just how much Jesus has already forgiven us. When it comes to forgiveness, Jesus is our model. To this day, I continue to ponder these unfathomable words He spoke from the cross: "Father, forgive them, for they do not know what they are doing" (Luke 23:34). If there ever was an undeserved gift, that was it! How could He forgive His murderers with His blood freshly dripping from His hands and His feet and His body in a slow state of suffocation?

Before sharing my own struggles with forgiveness, let's look at what forgiveness is not, what forgiveness does not mean. We don't want to be tripped up by misconceptions.

1. Forgiveness doesn't mean that what was done to you was somehow really "okay." It's not a denial of the depth of wrongness done.
2. Forgiveness doesn't mean you're required to return to a relationship with the one who hurt you. Although

forgiveness, by clearing the slate of wrongs, opens the door to reconciliation, one needs to be guided by the Lord. Being in an unsafe relationship isn't appropriate. Trust has to be earned and reestablished.

3. Forgiveness doesn't depend on your "feeling forgiving" but rather on a deep unyielding choice, a decision. It's a commitment to follow God's Word and the example Jesus set. Once forgiveness has occurred, feelings of forgiveness will eventually follow, especially as your heart becomes more healed.

4. Usually, forgiveness isn't an instantaneous event. It's normally an ongoing process because it takes time for our hearts to change. This is especially true if you need to continue to interact with the hurtful person or organization.

Now that we've looked at what forgiveness is not, let's consider what forgiveness is in addition to the Arnotts' definition. Think about these. Forgiveness means

- to pardon or excuse an offense without a penalty
- to grant relief from payment
- to cancel a debt
- to choose not to hurt those who have hurt you[2]

Oh, my friend, it's so much easier to write about forgiveness than it is to forgive! But forgiveness results in so many benefits that we must do it. It paves our way to wholeness, health, and freedom. Forgiveness is such a key area for all those involved with adoption.

My story is not what you think it's going to be. It's not about forgiving my birth parents or even my adoptive parents. My birth mother was always presented as a hero, a courageous young woman who gave me up for adoption for my good. (I totally understand that this may not be your case or your feelings. A lot of forgiveness may be needed.) I had to forgive my birth mom only for my identity struggle, for my sense of grief and loss, and for the shame I felt in being different and "less than." Forgiving this "hero" was not that difficult.

I also had to forgive my adoptive parents for making it difficult to talk about my birth mother, including who and where she might be. I couldn't risk bringing up the topic of possible contact lest I might hurt them. (I'm so glad adoptive parents now are guided to both share information about birth families and often, to have contact with them.)

> Forgiveness results in so many benefits that we must do it. It paves our way to wholeness, health, and freedom. Forgiveness is such a key area for all those involved with adoption.

My real struggle, my failure to forgive for years, came with my adopted brother, who was four years older than me. He was an angry person. It didn't take much for his "rage button" to be pushed, for him to scream obscenities, turn over objects, slam doors, or threaten me. My heart beat faster when he was around. All in all, it was difficult.

Even more than hating his angry behaviors, I hated what his anger did to me. It resulted in my becoming an extreme peacekeeper. The unpredictability of his next explosion kept both my parents and me in constant emotional turmoil. I saw my dad, normally a calm and gentle person, lose his cool and shout back when my brother had temper tantrums. Then my dad would experience hours of remorse. My mother was in the middle—sometimes on my dad's side, sometimes agreeing with my brother, but always torn between them. Miserable silences came during the aftermath of an anger episode, with everyone feeling awkward and depressed. Sometimes a whole day was wrecked.

The turmoil became unbearable, and inwardly, I decided not to create another ounce of stress for my family. I would just be super good, pleasing, helpful, and "happy" in order to guard their peace and survival. I shut down many of my own feelings and lost many aspects of the true me.

As my brother and I became more polarized in our emotions and behaviors, I was seen as the "good child" and he the "problem child." I hated that too. We made each other more extreme. I keenly felt his dislike of me and vice versa. Mostly, we avoided each other.

I felt helplessly shut down by him in other areas as well. Because he had difficulties on so many fronts, I tried to hide or minimize my successes. I got no joy from my straight A report card because he was getting Bs or Cs even though he had a higher IQ. I hid my excitement around my accolades in sports because he was so nearsighted and couldn't even participate. And on it went. I lived in conflict. On one hand I desperately wanted to find my own identity and sense of worth, but on the other hand I didn't want my positives to pour salt into my brother's wounds. This war within me raged on, keeping me torn and ragged. Either way I felt I'd lost.

Not until I was in my late teens did my parents share with me the tragic circumstances of my brother's early days. His birth mother, a schoolteacher, had left him alone while she worked. Neighbors repeatedly heard a baby screaming. He was eventually removed from his home by Social Services as he was severely neglected, hungry, angry, and distraught. Understanding his traumatic beginnings brought compassion. It gave me hope that someday I would be able to forgive him.

The hardest people to forgive are those who hurt us daily or repeatedly. That's where the Lord's help is desperately needed the most. I could not have even begun the process of forgiving my brother without Him.

Although I said prayers forgiving my brother during my teen years, I don't think I really forgave from my heart until I was in my twenties as I began to have a little distance and more perspective. Even then, some days I would forgive, but then I would want to take it all back. I was constantly asking the Lord for help. My prayer, "Help, Lord," must have sounded like a recorded announcement.

My floundering attempts to forgive came to a head soon after both of my parents died. Unknown to me at the time, my brother took a particular piece of our family furniture that had been verbally promised to me many times. He just took it. Feeling angry and betrayed, I prayed about it, somehow expecting the Lord to be "on my side." It was quite a shock when I sensed the Lord whisper, "Would you rather have a brother or that piece of furniture?" Put that way, I knew the answer. "Lord, I've got to have your help. I know I have to finish 'this' by forgiving him."

I began slowly, something like this:

- *Lord, I choose to give my brother the gift of forgiveness he doesn't deserve.* (I have to admit that when I started out, my thoughts were more on the "He doesn't deserve . . ." part, but I kept going.)
- *Lord, I forgive him for making my life miserable for so many years.*
- *Lord, I forgive him for his part in my decision to be a peacemaker and for losing myself in the process.*
- *Lord, I forgive him. . . .*

One afternoon, the dam broke, the dam that had been holding back my myriad "oughts" against my brother. What an ugly, powerful torrent rushed out. Nearly exhausted from the work of forgiving, I forced myself to keep on until the reservoir was drained. A strong sense of the Lord's presence had been with me through it all. It was done. At last, I felt clean inside. I knew I would never go back on this forgiveness.

What helped me reach this point? I was weary of feeling so stuck with this important relationship. I also believed God's promise to empower me. In addition, I'd matured in my understanding of God's Word and knew I needed to forgive in order for Him to forgive me (Mark 11:25). Last, I had learned an important truth—that unless I forgive, I can be tormented by the enemy (Matthew 18:34–35). Yes, I was experiencing this torment. I'd had enough and was ready to be free. I'd also matured enough and healed enough to recognize that some of the broken relationship was my own fault.

When my brother died in 2017, I was able to look back on many years of a good and peaceful relationship. The closeness and companionship seemed almost miraculous. I had learned to love him, and he me, and to love his remarkable wife as well. She and I remain friends.

Like me, you can find thousands of reasons not to forgive. It's so hard to do and can seem so unfair. But let me encourage you to press through. You can give the gift the other person doesn't deserve. And in the end, you'll find you've been given the bigger gift.

Freedom Prayer for All

If you've been praying the other Freedom Prayers, you will have worked through a lot of forgiveness already. However, this prayer addresses the issue of forgiveness itself.

Please read this entire freedom-giving prayer before praying it. Then pray the parts relevant for you, adding anything you think needs to be included and remembering to engage your heart.

Lord, it's so hard to forgive when people have truly hurt me. I've often just shut them out of my life. I've found ways to get back at them. I know that's not pleasing to you, and I greatly need your help.

*Please forgive me, because I know what your Scripture says about forgiveness. But I haven't always been willing to do it. Forgive me for holding on to grudges and for every ugly thing I've done to retaliate. Forgive me for justifying my position and hardening my heart toward people who have wounded me. Forgive me, too, for times I blamed you or judged you and cut you off because of the hurt I've re-*ceived. (Pause to receive God's forgiveness. Then based on His forgiveness, also forgive yourself.)

Lord, please soften my heart today and help me go deeper with my forgiveness. I choose to forgive both people and organizations I haven't yet forgiven. I choose to forgive _____ *for* _____. (Pause and ask the Holy Spirit to bring to mind people and organizations you've somehow not yet forgiven. Continue to forgive as you name them, specifically for the way each one hurt you.)

Like David in Psalm 51:10, I cry out, "Create in me a clean heart, O God; and renew a right spirit within me."[3]

Lord, please restore my relationship with the people I've forgiven. If this isn't appropriate, however, give me a right attitude toward them. In Jesus' name, amen.

PART THREE

EXPERIENCING WHOLENESS

We all want wholeness for ourselves and our children. Everywhere we turn on social media or in support groups, we hear of families struggling to raise foster and adopted children. Adult adoptees have, thankfully, educated parents about the needs of post-trauma children, but struggles remain.

Now that we understand the science of attachment, we're learning from counselors and therapies and using techniques to build attachment. Yet when we look around in our community, we still see many people suffering. Why is it still so hard? How do we find wholeness when confronted with all these challenging stories?

Perhaps we're still missing the central issue, the key that brings true healing and wholeness. Unless we understand redemption and are ready to embrace this idea in our families, the losses inherent in our lives don't make sense and maybe never will.

We may be striving to create an attached family, but what's also needed is deeper heart change in all of us. That can come only when we learn to see our families as a mercy, a gift, a redemption of loss. This is when we find wholeness.

A child who sees their adoptive family as a redemption is more likely to want to bond and attach. The relationship is less forced because both parties acknowledge the loss of the past but see the future as a gift of redemption. We can enter into a mystery, a mystery that teaches us that we're all beloved children of God and have been given the gift of a beautiful redemption story if we choose to receive it.

And that mystery begins with faith and prayer. Wholeness is found through an identity in something greater—through our creator, Father God. Using the power of prayer, we can find our way through the brokenness of foster care and adoption and "do something beautiful for God."[1]

Hear in his own words how this adoptee pressed into an identity in Christ to find wholeness.

ADOPTEE—TONY

A twenty-one-year-old woman became pregnant through an interracial relationship. While a multiethnic child wasn't accepted by many at the time, her convictions persuaded her that terminating her pregnancy was not an option. Fearing rejection by her family, she ran away and took up residence at a home for unwed pregnant women. At the birth, realizing she couldn't care for her newborn, she made the brave decision to turn her child over to foster care. I am that child.

This is where my journey began and God's presence in my life started to manifest itself before I even knew Him. Two years after entering the foster care system, a loving yet impoverished family invited me into their home and adopted me. I often questioned why my birth mother didn't take me home. I also wrestled with how my adoption made me different from children raised in their family of origin. I felt I was not accepted anywhere, mainly due to my ethnicity and adoption. This led to rebellion against my loving parents and brokenness. In my last year of college, as the only person in my family to attend and graduate from college, life questions resurfaced.

One day I picked up a Bible and began to read the New Testament. Then all my questions were answered. I said to myself, *This is who has been orchestrating my life! From my conception to my loving foster care, to my adoption in a family with a strong faith, throughout my poverty, and to my graduation from college.* I finally understood that my identity was not in "acceptance" of my ethnicity, birth, or adoption but in the Master Orchestrator of my life. While I've faced both challenges and opportunities and found success in my career, marriage, and later years, through it all I've steadfastly held on to my identity and purpose—a servant of Christ.

My Lord and my identity in Him is my forever foundation.

ELEVEN

REDEMPTION AND LIFE IN CHRIST

Let the redeemed of the LORD *tell their story—those he redeemed from the hand of the foe. — Psalm 107:2*

ADOPTIVE MOM—JODI

The airport hallway was crowded with people holding welcome signs and flowers. Everyone gathered nervously, straining to see the passengers coming from the terminal. A local news crew stood ready to film the amazing story of a fifteen-year-old boy about to be reunited with his sister after a five-year separation. She was my adopted daughter, and when we learned she had a brother left behind, we'd returned to her home country to find him.

It had been a long and grueling process. But today was the day all those years of waiting, all those tears cried, all those documents processed, all those obstacles overcome would finally be resolved. Her brother had been found, we'd adopted him, and he was arriving in America today.

As my new son and my husband rounded the bend in the corridor, their arms shot up in a wave. The welcome party let out a shout of joy, and my daughter began jumping up and down and weeping.

Every eye was fixed on my son's handsome face as he walked away from his life of trauma and into the arms of his waiting siblings. To quote the newscaster, "There was not a dry eye anywhere." My child's misery was being redeemed.

To be redeemed is to be reclaimed. To be made whole. To be restored in every possible way. Without the understanding of redemption, how can I hope to restore the loss that formed my family? But redemption makes it all whole and even glorious. Redemption changes everything. In redemption, I find a better way for life to turn out. I find the trials are replaced with grace and mercy and God's power to take the deepest sorrows of life and redeem them.

Christ is the central figure in the idea of redemption. The very gospel is based on redemption. Redemption means that which was broken, marred, full of sin and dysfunction has been redeemed by a God who loves us.

The crucifixion of Jesus was history's greatest sorrow. The Son of God had come to live among us, yet in our wickedness and hatred we chose to destroy Him. We killed the greatest Man who ever lived. We murdered the one who created us and loved us eternally. But He redeemed even that unimaginable loss. From the beginning to the end, the story of Jesus is a story of redemption upon redemption.

He redeemed the rejection of His birth, sent out to be born in a barn. He redeemed the sinners and the demon-possessed and the corrupt throughout His life on earth with His prayers and healing. And then He rose from the dead and redeemed it all—every last bit of it. His glorious resurrection made it all perfect.

Jesus is the author and finisher of redemption. If we can understand redemption, if we can truly grasp it and believe it and internalize its majesty, we can understand that our losses can also be redeemed. We don't need to live in a place of loss. We don't need to live with plan B. Our redeemed stories can be God's best.

The composition of my family was God's best for me. He saw the end from the beginning. When the day-to-day struggles of brokenness begin to overwhelm me and I feel pulled under the waves of turmoil, I remind myself that He is sovereign over my life. He lives in me, and He is good. He did not destine me for plan B. He destined me to be a living witness of the beauty of redemption. He destined me to let others see through me and our family that redemption is freely given if we embrace it.

This is the central healing that must take place in the adoption relationship. Can we accept that the redemption is providential and a gift from God, a mercy and a grace to be celebrated with joy?

Oh, how beautiful it is that God would redeem my situation by giving me a second chance with these children! Oh, what would I be without their teaching and enrichment in my life? Show me an adoptive parent, and I will show you a person who knows things about life and loss

Without the gift of redemption, I don't know how to make anything make sense for my adopted children.

and love. We have to open our hearts and our lives to the idea of redemption. We have to believe something even more beautiful can be made from all the loss inherent in adoption. We have to believe in redemption.

And those of us who follow Jesus believe it down to our very souls. He taught us what redemption is by His example of redeeming broken situations over and over again throughout His ministry on earth, and then ultimately He gave us the gift of redemption by rising from the dead and showing us the possibility of eternal life.

Without the gift of redemption, I don't know how to make anything make sense for my adopted children. I can't make sense of their deep and profound loss. I can't make sense of the neglect and abuse they suffered. I can't make sense of the torment brought on by one's very own family. I can't make sense of my own loss and why my life couldn't just have been "normal."

But oh, if I give my child and me the power of the idea of redemption, everything changes! Suddenly, reconciling these losses is not about making sense of how or why they happened, but about receiving as a gift the redemption given. I can't begin to explain or excuse what my children have been through, but I can point them to God's hand over their life to redeem that situation. Just as Christ redeemed me and gave me a new name—"beloved"—and a new identity when I was adopted into His family, my child has been given a redemption plan. They've been given a chance to open their heart and receive their adoption as a gift. When a child can find their way to this paradigm, to this belief, then plan B can feel like a beautiful outcome.

And my own life has been redeemed through the process of becoming an adoptive mother. I have seen my loss in infertility replaced with a glorious family built another way, a beautiful way. I have drawn so much closer to God through being an adoptive parent—through how it has stretched me and taken me outside of my own strength, needing the supernatural strength I get from knowing the Father. I see my own sins and sorrows of the past melt away as I wrestle with my precious children to help them overcome theirs. And I'm given the redemptive opportunity to make all things new not just for my children but for me as well. Each of us is given the gift of redemption and the glory of seeing a new purpose for our life. I can't imagine my life now without this most magnificent of gifts, the gift of adoption.

My journey as an adoptive mother has brought so much joy to my life. Seeing God's redemptive plans worked out in my children and seeing where they are today compared to where they might have been fills my heart with joy. Seeing my children able to give love and express love as adults fills me with joy. Seeing them take advantage of the opportunities they've been given and their desire to give back to the world is a great joy. Most of all, I have joy in knowing that I was obedient to the Lord and that He trusted me to parent these children. I also was chosen.

Please pause and pray about whatever is in your heart.

BIRTH MOM—LISA

One of my favorite verses in the Bible is Psalm 103:4, where David writes that the Lord "redeems your life from the pit and crowns you with love and compassion."

The Lord redeemed me and saved me from the pit. In the King James Version of the Bible, this pit is referred to as "destruction." Jesus lifted me out and saved me from destruction, but He didn't stop there. He crowned me with love and compassion, sometimes translated lovingkindness and tender mercies. I can't get over how beautiful this is. Not only does Jesus redeem us, but He also restores us from our brokenness.

Twenty-eight years after losing my son to adoption, one of my best friends called to tell me she and her husband were adopting two little boys from Ethiopia. I can only describe what happened next as a profound, spiritual experience.

> Not only does Jesus redeem us, but He also restores us from our brokenness.

The hard shell around my heart began to crack open. It seemed that perhaps adoption wasn't all bad. Maybe sometimes it was necessary. So many children needed families. It was so hard to see adoption as good, but if there was anything I loved, it was being a mother. I believed children were a gift from God and there was no limit on how much love I could give.

Russ and I prayed, wondering how it could be possible to see adoption in a new way. The answer seemed clear that this was where the Lord was leading us, and we began the process of also adopting two little boys from Ethiopia. This adoption soon grew to include a little girl we were sponsoring at an orphanage.

I still could not speak the word *adoption*, so I wrote *Ethiopia* on the folders containing our piles of paperwork. The idea that I would be an adoptive mom still threw me off balance, but I was ready to be a mom to children whose beautiful faces were still only in photos.

I already loved them.

Becoming an adoptive mom challenged everything I believed about adoption. Despite the injustice my son and I experienced, I could no longer hate it. My children were coming to me through this process, and my heart embraced them fully. I committed myself to honoring their first families and seeking as much connection with them as possible across the continents. I could not do to them what had been done to me. Not knowing if my child was doing well, was loved, or even alive was unspeakably cruel and devastating.

A year after arriving home with our three children, we returned to Ethiopia to adopt one more daughter. On that trip, we went on the greatest adventure of my life seeking relatives in remote areas. We found aunts and uncles, grandparents, and cousins, all overjoyed to hear about the children.

We gave them small albums with photos of the children and our contact information in the hope that one day we would hear from them. It was clear our children were loved by their families, and we wished they'd not been separated from them. But it was too late to change what happened. All we could do now was assure them of our great love for their children and make it as easy as possible for them to reach us.

In Psalm 40:2 David wrote, "He lifted me out of the slimy pit, out of the mud and mire; he set my feet on a rock and gave me a firm place to stand." Forgiveness and releasing bitterness allowed me to let go of the roots and vines I'd been clinging to in that slimy pit and be lifted out by the Lord. He gave me a firm place to stand, a place from which I could walk with confidence.

Sometimes I'm still surprised at the dramatic changes of heart and mind required for me to become an adoptive mom. Jesus didn't leave me trapped in the pit; He redeemed me. The Holy Spirit changed our hearts, giving us the willingness to move in a new direction.

My experience as a first mom makes me a better adoptive mom. My heart is for their first families. I wish more had been done to keep my adopted children from entering orphanages. Their families lost so much when their beautiful children left Ethiopia and found a new home with us in Idaho.

Our children's losses are many as well. They lost their extended families, language, culture, food, and more. At times they've wondered why God placed them in our family, and I understand that question. One of my children would have preferred being an only child. Another wishes he'd been adopted by a family steeped in athletics. Of course, none of us get to choose our families, but some adoptees feel this more acutely. Yet the Lord "sets the lonely in families" (Psalm 68:6). He chose us for our children and our children for us.

Brokenness and loss brought us together, launching us on a long healing journey. Being a first mom broke my heart and led me in desperation to Christ. Being an adoptive mom has challenged me far more than I expected. My failures and struggles can quickly pull me right back into shame. The enemy wants to drag me right back into that pit, but I won't go. I'm holding on to Jesus. And better yet, He's holding on to me. I am His beloved daughter.

My friend, whatever your role in adoption, the wounds may be great, but there is healing. The Lord redeems you from the pit and crowns you with love and compassion. Press on in hope, knowing the One who loves you more than you can even imagine has already done the work on the cross and won the battle. *Please pause and pray about whatever is in your heart.*

ADOPTEE—BETSY

A cold wet snowflake landed on my nose. For the last two hours I'd been standing outside in twenty-degree weather, waiting to go through the doors of a church. Inside, a glorious revival meeting was taking place. As I wiggled my toes to make sure they were still there, I was reflecting on the previous night's meeting. The atmosphere had been charged, electric. It felt like heaven was touching earth. The presence of God was so near, so real.

As we sang love songs to the Lord, I felt His liquid love surrounding me, filling my heart to overflowing. I couldn't stop trembling. It was like everything in my head about Father God leapt into my heart and kept leaping. Mighty waves of His love poured over me and into me and kept pouring. I was soggy, saturated, undone with His tangible love. All at once a ravenous hunger for Him was being filled.

Simultaneously, I experienced being overtaken by familiar phrases of Scripture. As it entered my heart, each phrase came alive. God knew me before the foundation of the world (Ephesians 1:4). He formed me in my mother's womb (Psalm 139:13). He has loved me with an everlasting love (Jeremiah 31:3). He will never leave me or forsake me (Hebrews 13:5). I will know the truth, and the truth will set me free (John 8:32). God has good plans and a good future for me (Jeremiah 29:11). All these words based on Scripture melted into one gigantic truth—my Father's great love for me.

As these words poured into my heart, a powerful new foundation for a Father-daughter relationship was being forged.[1] My life is not my own; I was bought with a price (1 Corinthians 6:20).

As these words penetrated my heart, I no longer wanted my life to belong to me but to the Lord.

For the joy set before Him, Jesus endured the cross (Hebrews 12:2). Father God had allowed Jesus, His only Son, to die an excruciating death to buy me back from my sin-filled state. Father God had my redemption in His mind from the beginning.

Instead of being some great theological truth I was supposed to fathom, the truth of my redemption was self-evident, easy. It was all very natural. God didn't want me to be separated from Him by my own sin, and I didn't want that either. *But Lord*, I thought, *what a cost*. And then I got it. The joy set before Him was me, my returning and belonging to Him.

When the church doors finally opened, I had snow on more than just my nose, but it didn't matter. My reflections continued with the Holy Spirit, my teacher, connecting the important dots of my life. God had bought me back for Himself. I belonged to Him, now and for eternity. I was embracing the bigger picture than just the facts of how the egg and sperm came together. How my life was physically formed was no longer that important.

Other facts also fell into second place. I carried a deep appreciation for my birth mother who refused to abort me when she heard God's voice. The tremendous love and devotion I had for my adoptive parents would always remain. These were truly the wonderful facts of my life, but I'd found an even greater truth, an eternal truth—that I belong to God my creator, my Father; to Jesus who bought me back; and to the indwelling Holy Spirit.

Out of my belonging to Him came my true identity, knowing who I really am. My identity was no longer up for grabs. It started with being God's daughter and expanded from there. How can I describe the peace, the sense of resolution I experienced? I know who I am!

For many years shame had tried to steal my true value. But I saw it now. The price Jesus was willing to pay for my redemption was proof of my value.

I had watched my parents delight and thrill at the way their children were different, but I couldn't receive it as a child. For example, my adoptive father had degrees from Princeton and Yale, and he was a college professor. And his son was gifted in mechanics. My father leaned into this and tried to extend himself to celebrate my brother's gifting that was so different from his own realm of familiarity. He celebrated, not just tolerated, things like working on a car with his son. He never gave up.

In the end, my brother was a godly man who stayed in his marriage and was good to his wife. My father understood what I came to learn.

The joy set before Christ was me, and it was you. For God's only Son, Jesus, paid the highest price for us both. He paid with every nail He allowed to pierce His raw and bleeding flesh. That's my value, and that's yours. Over the years, I'd received healing in the areas of abandonment, identity, and shame. But the revelation of the Father's love sealed my healing in a special, permanent way.

> God's only Son, Jesus, paid the highest price for us both. That's my value, and that's yours.

As a result, my prayer life changed from duty to delight, from obligation to friendship and awe. An overwhelming desire to live in God's presence filled my days. That was almost thirty years ago. Of course, life has had its ups and downs in those years, but my belonging, identity, and value issues have remained settled.

As my husband and I have served the Lord as ordained ministers, it's no longer been to prove myself, be the best, or be worthy of love and acceptance. Rather, it's come out of an entirely new motivation: I desire to give away the healing I've been given. I desire to help others find the reality of a loving God.

I'm still inspired by the results of one example of this desire to help others, which occurred with my birth mother, Virginia. As I mentioned, Virginia was a fine, tenderhearted, Christian woman, but she carried within herself all the marks of major shame.

Not long after I met her for the first time, my husband and I were leading a conference on healing, and I invited her and my half sister to attend as our guests. After asking and receiving Virginia's permission, I shared our story with the several-hundred-member audience. I focused on the strength she'd demonstrated as a teenager to listen to God's voice, resist the planned abortion, and go through an extremely lonely pregnancy feeling abandoned and rejected by her family. I focused on my birth mother's courage and generosity in placing me for adoption. I shared the feelings she experienced never knowing if I was "okay." Completely isolated from me, Virginia had wept over her loss on my birthdays and other special occasions. I was somewhere out in the great unknown instead of with her.

Then I asked her to stand and, along with my sister, to come to the front of the auditorium. She looked so lovely yet fragile as she faced an audience who now knew her deepest secret. She stood there, unsure of what would come next. I didn't know either. We were tied together, trembling, in a moment of confession and vulnerability.

Then the unexpected happened. The place erupted. People stood to their feet, clapping and shouting, "Hurrah, Virginia! We love you!" Then spontaneously, many gathered around her, hugging her, praising her, and thanking her. The deepest, dreaded secret of her life, which she'd not even shared with her other children, was now open to the world, and she was being loved, accepted, and embraced. It was a healing moment, a moment of life-changing transformation.

I tangibly felt the Lord's pleasure at all that had taken place. Glancing at Virginia as we were leaving the auditorium, I noticed the hard lines of shame in her face had begun to soften. She walked with her head held high, her eyes looking straight ahead, ready to meet life head-on.

God has many ways of restoring His children!

Today, I've found joy in being an adopted person. I feel specially chosen. I feel like I brought something to my adoptive family that was cherished. My interests and giftings expanded my family. And the faith I was introduced to has been substantial enough to carry me through life. I can see that the same God who was faithful to my parents has also been faithful to me. My parents' love was consistent even when I was failing. They never turned their backs on me, and I knew I could always go home.

In thinking about your own life, it's not necessary to go to a revival for your deepest issues to be healed (although that was a significant step in my own pathway). God has many different pathways to His healing presence and healing truth.

Please pause and pray about whatever is in your heart.

In the next chapter, we share a variety of healing prayers. May you find His healing presence as you encounter Him through these prayers.

TWELVE

GOING DEEPER IN HEALING PRAYER

It is for freedom that Christ has set us free. —Galatians 5:1

The following Going Deeper prayers are presented to eliminate the pressure of generational influences, abolish lies and replace them with God's truth, heal hurts and wounds, and defeat your enemy by removing his influence.

Sometimes, however, a person may pray through all these areas but still have what seems like an unexplained instability. For example, they may seem positive for a while, but then give in to negative behaviors, often self-sabotaging. When this is the case, they may still be carrying a "shattered" heart with two or more pieces. When this is true, it's appropriate to look for trauma that occurred with their birth family, while being carried in the womb, or during their early years (from birth to age six). It's also possible for the effects of trauma to be exacerbated when there's been a strong occult influence in the family.

As always, Jesus can bring healing and wholeness. In fact, in Luke 4:18, He's reading from Isaiah 61 that says, "He has sent

---

This chapter—written by Betsy—shares approaches and prayers that can help you and/or your child in the journey toward greater wholeness.

Me to heal the brokenhearted" (NKJV). The Greek translated "broken"—*syntetrimmenous*—is also easily translated as "broken in pieces" or "shattered." We see this in Revelation 2:27: "He will shatter them like pottery" (CSB). And to paraphrase Luke 4:18, "He has sent me to heal the shattered heart."

If you still observe instability after praying through the deeper prayers, please consider seeking professional help from a Christian minister or counselor trained specifically to set the stage for Jesus to come and bring unity and consolation into the shattered heart.[1]

These Going Deeper prayers are an invitation to you. Of course, you may choose to not use them, but we want to encourage you to read them with an open heart along with the additional explanations and guidelines. Listen to the Lord as to what He would have you do.

We also acknowledge that our readers come from many different faith backgrounds, and some of these prayers may be new prayer approaches for you. We encourage you to be open to new understanding about the provision of healing and freedom Jesus has secured for us.

These prayers are meant to undergird you and/or your child and to come alongside and strengthen the effective approaches you're already using. Our heartfelt desire is that these prayers will be an important part in your becoming more healed, whole, and free.

"But what can I do about others who also need healing?" you may ask. As you've read this book, we trust that God has highlighted areas He wants to heal in everyone involved in your adoption story. But you are only one person. What should you do? We recommend three things:

1. Let healing begin with you. We encourage you to talk with God, praying all the prayers relevant to your role in previous chapters as well as those yet to come in this

chapter. As the Lord does His work in your life, trust that He will also be working in the lives of those connected to you.

2. As a reminder, if you're a birth or adoptive parent and your child is under ten or particularly immature for their age, we suggest that you pray over them while they're asleep. Again, this is just as effective and easier for both of you. Your child doesn't have to say the prayers for you to see God working in their life.

3. As God leads you, share what you've learned with others in your adoption constellation, even if it looks like everything is okay. Don't just hand this book over. Offer to go through it together.

Before you dive into these prayers, there's one more important topic to discuss: hearing God's voice.

"I don't know if I've ever heard His voice," you might say. Others would agree with you. Most of us have to learn to hear God's voice. But the Bible assures us that hearing His voice is a normal part of our relationship with Jesus. He Himself said, "My sheep hear my voice" (John 10:27 CSB).

We're not referring to hearing an audible voice, but rather to hearing God through "sensing" or having an "impression" of what He's saying/doing/communicating. It's likely that you're already hearing His voice, but perhaps you're not recognizing it. You may be "hearing" His voice in several ways, such as a Bible verse "jumping off the page" while you're reading Scripture, or seeing a picture in your mind/spirit, or experiencing an impression or feeling, especially when you're focusing on the Lord.

If you're uncertain about whether you're hearing the Lord, please don't be discouraged. Even the great prophet Samuel had to learn to hear His voice (1 Samuel 3:3–10). See the Helpful

Resources section at the end of this book for excellent resources on this topic.

When you're praying, asking to hear God, remember this can happen in a number of different ways as noted above. You may sense His presence, hear/sense/see Jesus "speaking" to you, or directly experience His love. You may see pictures, which is a common way we communicate with Him. However you interact with God, you can expect your life to be changed.

As you start to go through the following prayers, be expectant and open to "hearing" His voice communicate with your heart, even if it's for the very first time.

Going Deeper in Prayer for Generational Influences

Although we haven't presented a specific chapter on negative generational influences in this book, it's a significant topic we've mentioned. We can give ourselves as well as our adopted child a gift by praying prayers that break negative generational influences whether they come from their first or adoptive family.

While the generational influences/curses are direct from the first family, the adopted child is also significantly affected by their second family in both positive and negative ways. While they don't directly inherit the generational influences of their second family, once they're a legal member of the family, they can be majorly impacted by their issues. For instance, if their family carries issues of anger and violence, the child will likely carry issues of anger and violence as well. So it's wise to go through the process and break negative family influences from both families.

Let's, however, find the balance and now look at generational inheritance from the positive side. Generational influences were designed by God to impart blessing through our family's inheritance. Exodus 20:6 teaches that God shows love to up to a thousand generations of those who love Him and keep His commands. He intends that the family line should function as a conduit for blessings to flow from generation to generation. The anointing, giftings, and blessings received by our parents, etc., are meant to be passed along through the generations and to increase every time they are imparted. It has been said that one generation's ceiling should be the next generation's floor, because the benefits of each generation are meant to build upon those of the previous generations.[2]

We see negative characteristics coming down a generational line the same way we see giftings and blessings. Have you ever developed a genogram to look at your entire family and observe its characteristics? Or have you ever filled out a doctor's questionnaire, checking off all the illnesses that occurred in your family line? Why is this important information? Because there's a strong likelihood that you may have the same illnesses or at least a predisposition or vulnerability to them. (You'll find a list of negative characteristics commonly occurring in adoption on pages 203–204.)

Now, this discussion about generational influences may be a new area of thought for you. If so, please take time to consider it in light of Scripture. In the Old Testament, it's clear that God sees us within the context of our family lines as well as individually. In the Bible, He's often referred to as the "God of Abraham, Isaac and Jacob" (Exodus 3:16; Acts 3:13; 7:32). He also called Himself that when He appeared to Moses through the burning bush (Exodus 4:5). And He even called the priests to serve Him according to their family line. Family lines are important to God.

To better understand generational family patterns, let's look further into the Scriptures.

Scriptures

The second commandment is an important place to start:

> Do not bow in worship to them [idols], and do not serve them; for I, the LORD your God, am a jealous God, bringing the *consequences* of the fathers' *iniquity* on the children to the third and fourth generations of those who hate me.

> Exodus 20:5 CSB, emphasis added

The word *iniquity* not only speaks of actual sin but includes the principle of having a strong tendency or a predisposition to sin. In the second commandment, God is establishing a curse that the children will experience a "pressure" to sin in the same way their fathers (and mothers) did. In other words, as their family line. The consequence of the iniquity is a pressure on each of us to repeat our family's unrighteous patterns. It's as if an invisible hand is on our shoulder, pushing us in the same direction our ancestors traveled. This consequence/pressure continues until some descendant recognizes the operation of the iniquity curse and applies the provision of the cross to repent of the sin and bring the curse to an end. You will have an opportunity to do this in this Going Deeper prayer.

When we each think of our family inheritance, most of us fail to realize that we receive an emotional and spiritual inheritance as well as a physical inheritance. We inherit more than our appearance, the family furniture, and the house. We also inherit negative family patterns that are repeated in consecutive generations. These might include drug abuse, sexual sin or abuse, anger and violence, criminality, or addictions or fears to give a few examples. Again, what is in your family line that you're determined to not repeat? Is this a continuing struggle for you?

In John 9:1–2 we see a story that illustrates how prevalent the understanding of this principle was during New Testament times: "As [Jesus] was passing by, he saw a man blind from birth. His disciples asked him, 'Rabbi, who sinned, this man or his parents, that he was born blind?'" (CSB). How direct is that? They asked Jesus about the source of the blindness, about whether generational influences were at work. In their culture it was understood that inheritance includes everything our family line carries.

See if there is fresh revelation about receiving freedom from generational influences for you in the following Scriptures.

This passage in Leviticus expresses the principle that God requires us to confess (acknowledge) our own sins as well as the sins of our fathers and to humble ourselves so that we may receive His remedy—His sacrifice on the cross:

> But when they confess their iniquity and the iniquity of their ancestors . . . and when their uncircumcised hearts are humbled and they make amends for their iniquity, then I will remember my covenant with Jacob. I will also remember my covenant with Isaac and my covenant with Abraham, and I will remember the land.
>
> Leviticus 26:40–42 CSB

In the books of Daniel, Nehemiah, and Ezra, we can read prayers where each man applied the principles expressed in Leviticus 26:40, confessing the sins of their fathers and humbling themselves. Great victories and freedom came forth from these prayers (Daniel 9:4–20; Nehemiah 9–10; Ezra 9:6–15). (Please note that we're not blaming our ancestors but simply confessing the sin patterns that existed in their lives.)

First John 1:9 promises us that if we confess the sin and turn from it, God will forgive us and cleanse us from all unrighteousness.[3]

The wonderful news is that you can put an end to these influences by applying the work of the cross. In Galatians 3:13–14, the

Bible tells us Jesus became a curse for us that we might receive the blessings of Abraham. We can find freedom for ourselves, the generations that follow us, and our adopted children.

It's unfortunate that some people don't receive the gift of freedom from the pressure of generational influences. They've been taught that Jesus has already dealt with these effects at the cross. While this is true, an implied conclusion says we don't need to do anything further to be free of these patterns. There is, however, a big difference between Jesus' providing that freedom for us and our receiving that freedom.

Just as we have to receive salvation by faith, we also have to receive our freedom from the pressure of generational family patterns by faith. The prayers offered in this book are designed to help us confess and forgive so we're positioned to receive God's healing and freedom, including freedom from generational family patterns.

Let's dig deeper to understand how all this works.

Sin (sinful acts) results in curses (penalties or negative consequences). For example, if you drive 70 miles an hour in a 55-mile-an-hour zone, you're breaking the law. If you're caught, you may receive a stiff penalty or fine, the curse or negative consequence of your sin. While we might not be caught breaking a man-made law here on earth, we're always "caught" when we break one of God's laws.

When Jesus died on the cross, He died not only for our sins but for all the curses (negative consequences/penalties) that resulted from those sins. The provision was made for the entire sin slate to be totally cleared. What a gift He gave us.

Again, Galatians 3:13–14 makes it clear that Jesus became a curse on our behalf so that we might receive the blessings of Abraham. If you're a believer, in a covenant relationship with God, you have this covenant blessing.

So is it enough to know this? Yes and no. The yes is obvious. How wonderful that Jesus' sacrificial death provided for the cleansing of our sin and the curses, for salvation, for physical healing, and for our freedom. But this is where the no answer comes in. We may not receive the fullness of what God has for us because we don't know how.

This is where the Going Deeper prayer will help you know what to do.

Which Generational Influences?

You're now ready to start preparing for the Going Deeper prayer process. But wait. From which generational influences do you need to gain freedom? Which generational influences do you want to include as you go through the prayer process?

We'll keep it simple and focus only on adoption issues.

Begin by developing a list of possible generational influences. In order to do that, consider the areas you've already prayed about through using the Freedom Prayers: abandonment, grief and loss, and shame. If these emotions seem particularly negative and strong and you see them in your family line, include them on your list. Also, unworthiness frequently goes hand in hand with shame. And since it's likely that you've experienced it somewhere in the adoption process, trauma may be in your family line.

What about sexual sin? Sex outside of marriage or adultery may have occurred. And deception? Lying, cheating, and secretiveness are common in adoptive children and are often in family lines. What else do you think might be affecting you or your child? Even if you don't know your or your child's family history, you can look at the struggle areas. These are strong indicators of possible generational influences at work. Also, don't forget to ask the Holy Spirit to reveal what else is important to include.

Here is your starting list:

- abandonment
- addictions

- abuse
- "abnormal" grief and loss
- shame, unworthiness
- trauma
- sexual sins, sex outside of marriage, adultery
- deception, lying, cheating, secretiveness
- _____
- _____

A gift adoptive parents can give to their child as well as to themselves is to stop the effects of negative generational influences. They pressure children to repeat the same family patterns their birth family displayed.

Now, read the following prayers and Prayer Steps before you pray them. Make sure you understand the process, and then ask the Lord to help you pray from your heart and with faith. The reality of generational influences will become more personal as you prepare. Last, of course, use the pronoun that fits your child.

Initial Prayer

Lord, the last thing I want is to continue the generational sin patterns and negative influences that have plagued my family line. I don't want them for myself or for my children. Give me wisdom and revelation about how to pray for my adopted/foster child. I need to know what generational influences to address to bring them freedom. I yearn for true righteousness. Free me now so I can grow closer to your heart. In Jesus' name, amen.

Prayer Steps for Generational Influences

Lord, I confess the sins of my ancestors, my parents, and my own sin of _____. (Name each item on your generational influence list. Note: We're not blaming or judging others but rather confessing their past sins. It's particularly important to do this if we ourselves have entered into them.)

Lord, I choose to forgive my ancestors as well as anyone else who has influenced me to enter into these same sins and the resulting curses. (Pause and specifically forgive those setting you up for these sins.)

Please forgive me, Lord, for entering into my ancestors' sins, iniquity, and curses and making them my own. (Pause and receive God's forgiveness.) *And on the basis of your forgiveness, I choose to forgive myself.* (Now forgive yourself.)

I renounce the sins and curses of _____. (Name each item in your list again.)

Lord, I break these powers and pressures from my life. I also break them off my descendants, including all adopted children, through the work of Christ on the cross. I receive God's freedom from the sins and resulting curses. I receive _____. (Pause and receive blessings from the Lord. Quiet yourself and listen for His voice. You may receive Scripture, or thoughts, or pictures from Him. Then record these so you can meditate on them later.)[4]

Closing Prayer

Lord, I'm thankful for what you've done today and for your presence. Thank you for freeing me from the pressure of generational influences and enabling me to walk in a godlier way. Let the issues of abandonment, shame, and unworthiness be settled. Let me know my value and begin to see myself as you see me.

I cancel any attempted backlash or counterattack from the kingdom of darkness. Let your grace enable me to stand strong against any future attacks of the enemy. I pray that I will have a growing relationship with you, particularly in experiencing your Father's heart to a greater and greater degree. Thank you that I have a safe place with you as I grow in my freedom.

In Jesus' name, amen.

Now congratulate yourself for pressing through. You may want to take a little time before engaging in the next deeper prayer.

Going Deeper in Prayer for Confronting Lies

It's not enough to identify lies and then start declaring the truth. It's more effective to take responsibility for believing them and all the negative effects they've had. We also need to forgive anyone, including ourselves, who helped us form these lies. And because they've been such a strong influence, we need to formally break agreement with each one of them.

After forgiveness, we can cancel agreement with each lie. We can then receive and declare God's truth about ourselves, others, and God Himself, receiving new and positive truths and beliefs to replace the old lies.

This is a useful arena in which to hear God's voice. It's okay to ask the Lord to show you the truth He wants you to believe. He's been waiting for you to ask Him. Be prepared to write down the truth and meditate on it for thirty days. (We're told it takes twenty-one days to form a new habit, so let's be sure your new truth becomes a strong habit.) Last, use the pronoun that fits your child.

To help you get started, we've included a number of lies we find among people involved in adoption. Select any to which you relate.

Adoptive parent lies:

- It's my job to make up for any lack/losses my child experienced before adoption.
- I'm a failure because my child hasn't bonded with me.

- I made a mistake adopting since my child needs more help than I can provide.
- My child's identity started being formed the day I adopted them. (When *did* it start?)
- My child's acting out makes me a bad parent.
- I'll never be able to find a peaceful relationship with my child's birth mom/family.
- (Add any other lies you believe regarding adoption.)

Birth mother lies:
- I will always be in pain from the loss of my child.
- I can never forgive those who abandoned me when I needed their help to keep my child.
- I will always feel _____ because I gave my child up for adoption. (Fill in the negative emotion that has you trapped.)
- After what I've done, I need to compensate by being a super mom to the children I do have (or will have).
- (Add any other lies you believe regarding adoption.)

Adoptee lies:
- I am a mistake.
- I will never know who I really am.
- I am unlovable.
- There's something wrong with me.
- No matter how hard I try, I will never be as good as other people.
- My best solution is to find something to numb my pain.
- I will always be angry.
- Since I have been victimized, I have a right to hurt other people.
- (Add any other lies you believe regarding adoption.)

Once you've selected some of these lies and asked the Holy Spirit which ones to add, you're ready to use the following prayers and go through the Prayer Steps. Please read through the prayer and Prayer Steps as well as the example and hints we've included, then ensure that you can pray the words from your heart and with faith. It's time to start reducing the number of lies operating in your life.

Initial Prayer

Lord, in Romans 12:2, you tell me to not let my mind agree with the culture around me but to be transformed by the renewing of my mind so I will know your perfect will for my life. I willingly choose to enter into this transformation process. I want to be free of the crippling influence of every lie I've believed. Lead me now as I take action to get these lies out of my life.
In Jesus' name, amen.

Prayer Steps for Abolishing Lies

Please repeat these steps for each lie you want to replace with God's truth.[5]

1. *Lord, I confess that I've believed the lie that* _____.
   (Name the lie.)
2. *I forgive those who have contributed to my receiving and believing this lie.* (Pause and forgive specific people.)
3. *Lord, please forgive me for believing this lie and for all the ways I've let it hurt my life as well as hurt others.* (Pause and receive God's forgiveness.)
4. *Lord, because you forgive me, I choose to forgive myself for believing this lie and for its negative effects in my life.* (Now forgive yourself.)

5. *I renounce and break my agreement with this lie and with every way it has opened the door to the kingdom of darkness.* (Pause and ask the Lord what truth He wants you to believe rather than the old lie. The Holy Spirit is faithful to communicate to you what God would have you believe. You can confirm the truth by ensuring that it agrees with what God says in His Scripture. Write down the truth to use for the next step as well as for the Follow-Up—see below.)

6. *I now receive and accept the truth that* _____. (Declare your new truth out loud.)[6]

Closing Prayer

Thank you, Lord, for exposing the lies that have trapped me and for helping me to abolish them today. I thank you for giving me the necessary discipline to meditate upon and plant your truths deep into my heart and mind. In Jesus' name, amen.

Hints for Writing Your New Truths

- Make sure the truth addresses the main issue the lie represents. It should counteract the essence of the lie.
- Generally, the truth is the opposite of the lie. It expresses God's way of looking at the same concept or belief that's revealed by the lie. It must agree with the principles of Scripture and God's character.
- When needed, include a phrase such as "by God's grace" or "with His help."

Example:

- Lie: I will always be lonely.
- Truth: With God's help, I will begin to reach out to others and also receive from them. He has designed me to fit into His family.

Follow-Up

It's important to diligently meditate upon your new truth for each of the next thirty days so it will be well implanted in your mind and heart as well as in new neural pathways in your brain. Great job. Freedom is on the way. Can you sense it? Give yourself a break before going deeper with hurts and wounds.

Going Deeper in Prayer for Healing Hurts and Wounds

This approach to healing prayer enables you to be healed by being in the presence of Jesus and/or by what He says or does. As we noted in chapter 8, the lives of many individuals were transformed as Jesus spoke to them. We mentioned the woman at the well, who was deeply shamed but radically changed into a fervent evangelist through her encounter with Jesus. Also, the words Jesus spoke to the woman caught in adultery spared her from death and set her free to begin a new, sinless life. When Jesus speaks to our hearts, the deepest wounds can be healed.

Please refer back to the introduction to this chapter if you would like to review the section on hearing God's voice. We want to encourage you to be expectant that He will communicate with you as you go deeper to receive healing of the hurts and wounds of your heart. Hearing God's voice will help you receive His healing.

As you prepare, find a quiet place where you won't be interrupted. You may even need to let family members know you're unavailable.

Start by taking time to meditate on just how well God knows you and cares for you. This is powerfully illustrated in these passages from the book of Psalms:

Lord, you know everything there is to know about me. You perceive every movement of my heart and soul, and you understand my every thought before it even enters my mind. You are so intimately aware of me, Lord. You read my heart like an open book and you know all the words I'm about to speak before I even start a sentence! You know every step I will take before my journey even begins. You've gone into my future to prepare the way, and in kindness you follow behind me to spare me from the harm of my past. You have laid your hand on me! This is just too wonderful, deep, and incomprehensible! Your understanding of me brings me wonder and strength.

Psalm 139:1–6 TPT

Wherever I go, your hand will guide me; your strength will empower me. It's impossible to disappear from you or to ask the darkness to hide me, for your presence is everywhere, bringing light into my night.

Psalm 139:10–11 TPT

God is so present with you and so ready to bring healing to your heart, as you ask Him.

Please read through this complete healing prayer description and make sure you're clear on the procedure before you start.

Initial Prayer

Lord, I thank you that you know me so well. You know the gifts and strengths you put into my life and the passions of my heart. You also know every time my heart has been bruised or broken. Thank you that I am safe with you and don't have to pretend or hide my brokenness from you.

Right now, in Jesus' name, I bind the enemy from every attempt to distract me, confuse me, or try to keep me from hearing your voice.

Lord, thank you for your blood. I trust you to be my protector, my shield. You are my Great Physician. Be with me now as you reveal the hurt you want to heal. In Jesus' name, amen.

Prayer Steps for Healing Hurts and Wounds

Please repeat this ministry procedure using these prayer steps for each hurt God reveals.[7]

1. **Identifying the memory:** *Lord, I ask you to reveal a painful event or memory you want to heal.* Don't try to think up something. Just wait several minutes and let a memory come to you. If nothing comes, however, it's okay to choose a hurtful event you know needs healing. But we recommend that you not choose your deepest hurts while you're learning this approach.

2. **Settling in:** Once a painful event or memory comes, take a little time to "be there" and become aware of the details. Note where you are, who's there, what's happening, and how you feel.

3. **Inviting Jesus to join you:** *Jesus, I invite you to join me in this memory. Thank you for being here with me and helping me be in contact with you.* Jesus promises to always be with you. So ask Him to show you that He was with you at the time the painful event occurred. You might sense His presence in any number of ways. You may "see" Him, "feel" Him, or just "know" He's with you. Where is He? What is He doing or saying to you at the time of your painful event? Have a conversation with Him if you'd like.

4. **Releasing pain:** *Lord, I give you each one of the painful emotions I'm experiencing. I give you _____.* Name and give each negative feeling to the Lord. Continue releasing each negative feeling until you're finished. Take your time.

5. **Forgiveness:** *Lord, I choose to forgive _____ for what they did to me in this experience.* Name the person or persons causing the pain. Repeat this step with other people until your heart feels at peace.

6. **Healing:** *Jesus, please heal my heart from all the effects of this experience.* As you ask Him to heal your heart, wait and sense or see what He says or does.

Closing Prayer

Lord, thank you for healing my heart and for your ongoing care and healing. It should be easy for gratitude to flow from your heart to God as you realize that you've just experienced an encounter with Him that brought healing no man could give you.

Hints for Receiving Your Healing

- Jesus will always speak in ways that are kind, compassionate, or gently corrective. If you hear something harsh or condemning, it's not the real Jesus speaking. In this case, it's best to wait and thoroughly pursue this deeper level of healing with an experienced minister or counselor.

- Although Jesus' healing doesn't erase the facts of your painful experience, it does, however, totally reframe it. You will likely now see the experience from His perspective. The pain is removed, and His peace comes.

- Unforgiveness can often block your sensing the Lord. If you're not able to sense Him, forgive others and ask God to forgive you. Then go back to step 1.

- Sometimes it's easier to forgive others after you've received the healing. If you're struggling to forgive others, you may reverse steps 5 and 6. In fact, sometimes the best approach is to alternate between steps 5 and 6 several times until both the forgiveness and healing are complete.

- If you know your heart is "shattered" from past trauma, contact a minister or counselor experienced in this area to guide you.[8]

You are on a solid pathway to healing. That's wonderful. You can enter into this kind of healing many times until you know your heart is restored.

Going Deeper in Prayer for Defeating the Enemy

Would you be shocked if we told you that the list of ways Satan, our enemy, tries to oppress and destroy us could fill an entire book? Unfortunately, this is true. He enters our lives in a number of ways. These include personal sin, emotional trauma, severe illness or accidents, involvement with the occult, going into a passive state of mind (trance), and demonic forces coming from the sins of past generations.

Satan and his helpers—the kingdom of darkness—try to prevent us from being saved, harass us once we are saved, and keep us from fulfilling our complete destiny in God. His strategies are subtle. Satan doesn't play fair. He tries to prevent us from taking him seriously or even thinking he's real.

Most often he works through our minds by bringing negative thoughts such as *I am such a failure as a parent*. The problem is we think this thought is our own. He can also affect us by causing nightmares, insomnia, physical pain, the compulsion to cut, suicide fantasies, and addictions, to name a few. He and his demons often intensify our emotions so they are excessive and exaggerated compared to normal emotions.

He can also cause an emotion to continue for much longer than normal, such as prolonged grief. He can affect us physically, emotionally, mentally, and spiritually. The bottom line is that it's time to get him out of your life and out of your child's life.[9]

It's time to stop ignoring the kingdom of darkness and go on the offense about this real enemy. It's time to forgive those who may have misled you about this important area. We could share many dramatic "before and after" deliverance stories, but it's more important for you to focus on the truth of what Scripture says about your enemy.

A major key to ousting the kingdom of darkness is to know the authority God has delegated to you as His child. Evicting your enemy is a matter of walking in your authority and, in Jesus' name, commanding your enemy to leave. Actually, we're commanding out Satan's workers, which the Bible calls "demons."

Here are some relevant Scriptures God has provided to help us decide to live the overcomer's life.

Scriptures

Jesus' Defeat of Satan

Then Jesus made a public spectacle of all the powers and principalities of darkness, stripping away from them every weapon and all their spiritual authority and power to accuse us. And by the power of the cross, Jesus led them around as prisoners in a procession of triumph. He was not their prisoner; they were his!

Colossians 2:15 TPT

For this purpose the Son of God was manifested, that He might destroy the works of the devil.

1 John 3:8 KJ21

God anointed Jesus of Nazareth with the Holy Ghost and with power, and ... He went about doing good and healing all who were oppressed by the devil, for God was with him.

Acts 10:38 KJ21

Jesus Promises Both Authority and Protection to Believers

Jesus replied, "While you were ministering, I watched Satan topple until he fell suddenly from heaven like lightning to the ground. Now you understand that I have imparted to you my authority to trample over his kingdom. You will trample upon every demon before you and overcome every power Satan possesses. Absolutely nothing will harm you as you walk in this authority."

Luke 10:18–19 TPT

Jesus Partners with Believers to "Cast Out" Demons

These signs will accompany those who have believed: in My name they will cast out demons.

Mark 16:17 NASB

Satan's Final Destination

And fire came down from heaven and devoured them. And the devil who deceived them was thrown into the lake of fire and brimstone.

Revelation 20:9–10 NASB

Which Demons?

We're now ready to start preparing for the process of deliverance. But we have a problem. Just as with generational influences, we have a question that needs an answer. What exactly are we going to "cast out"? Which demons do we want to evict?

Just as we did with generational influences, we'll keep it simple and focus on adoption issues.

You can start with the same list you developed for the generational-influences prayers and other adoption issues. It's possible that sin and curses have enabled demons to further harass and oppress you or your child through each of the items on the list.

Check out each one to see if it needs to be on the prayer list for defeating the enemy. You can tweak the list as needed. Let's start again with abandonment, grief and loss, and shame. Think about whether you experience these emotions in an exaggerated way or they've lasted longer than normal. Ask the Holy Spirit if they've become demon influenced. Then ask the same questions for trauma, sexual sin, sex outside of marriage, and

adultery. Go on through the rest of the list. Then ask the Holy
Spirit to show you what else He suggests you add to your list.
    Here is your starting list:

- abandonment
- "abnormal" grief and loss
- shame, unworthiness
- trauma
- sexual sins, sex outside of marriage, adultery
- deception, lying, cheating, secretiveness
- _____
- _____

Hints before Engaging in Deliverance

Before you begin,

- repent of any known sin in your life (ask God's help to
  stop doing it)
- meditate on Scriptures about your authority as a
  believer
- consider connecting with someone experienced in deliverance to help you

Once more, if praying for a child under the age of ten, you
can do this on their behalf while they're asleep. This is an easy
approach and just as effective.

Deliverance Process

Caution: If you feel concerned about your ability to do self-
deliverance, or if you or your family line have had much involvement in the occult, find someone experienced in deliverance to
walk through this with you at least for the first time or two.

Please, as usual, read through the following prayers and Prayer Steps. Once you're clear about the process, you can take your list of demons and proceed.

Initial Prayer

Lord, I thank you that you haven't left me defenseless against Satan or his demons. You've delegated your authority to me to command him out of my life and my child's life in your name. I choose to embrace the authority you've given me. In Jesus' name, I bind every demon that would try to bring fear, confusion, or unbelief about my authority.

Lead me now, Holy Spirit, as I use my authority as a believer to defeat my enemy. In Jesus' name, amen.

Prayer Steps for Defeating the Enemy

Please make sure you've done step 1 for each demon on your list before doing steps 2 and 3.[10]

1. **Confession and forgiveness:**
   - *I confess my sin or sins done against me leading to* _____. (Insert name of demon.)
   - *I forgive all who have influenced me or sinned against me in the area of* _____. (Be specific about who needs to be forgiven for the specific sin.)
   - *I repent of every way I've opened the door for the enemy to come in and influence my life.* (Pause and receive God's forgiveness. Then based on His forgiveness, forgive yourself.)
2. **Renouncing:** *In the name of Jesus, I renounce and break all agreements with the demons on my list.*
3. **Commanding:** *I take authority over the demon of* _____, *and I command you to leave me and my child now in Jesus' name and in my authority as a*

believer. (Command each demon on your list to leave, one at a time, pausing with each one to sense/verify that it has gone before continuing.)

Closing Prayer

Lord, I thank you for helping me get the enemy out of my life. I bind any remaining demons in the name of Jesus and tell them they cannot operate in my life and will eventually be cast out. I also dismantle and cancel every planned counterattack against me or my child. I command each demon assigned to carry out a counterattack to be turned over to Jesus.

Lord, I ask for your blood to be my protection. Thank you for new freedom as you have given me victory over the enemy today. In Jesus' name, amen.

Congratulations. You didn't let intimidation hold you back. May you continue to walk in your God-given authority and defeat your enemy.

CONCLUSION

Beloved, you have finished this book. We celebrate you and your courage to seek healing. You have acknowledged the pain and opened the door of your heart to be healed, and we believe our Lord Jesus will fill you with joy as you experience His redemptive love over your life.

Adoption is the experience God used to propel each of us into the life we have now. A life redeemed by Him and purposed by Him. We three authors have shared our journeys—victories as well as places of agonizing distress where God met us. Often, out of His goodness, He found us in ways and at times we least expected it. Some of these were truly "out of our box." We know He will do the same for you.

We've also shared the journeys of others in the adoption constellation with different backgrounds and stories. No two families or adoption stories are the same, but the God we know is *always* the same, and He will meet every one of us because of His great love.

We commend you for accepting our invitation to enter into this prayer journey. We know you've been stretched, but our prayer is that you have also truly benefited. Let these prayers become your own tools as you move ahead in life.

Whether you're in a place of great success and victory or in the dregs of discouragement, look to God to provide what you need. Continuing to pray healing prayers is the most vital part of your healing. We are later in our journeys than most of you, and we can promise that joy is found after healing. Even the most broken parts of your life can become places of wholeness and redemption.

However your life has been impacted by adoption, God passionately cares about you and your future. He is present to be all that you need.

With His blessings and ours as well,

Betsy, Lisa, and Jodi

ACKNOWLEDGMENTS

From Betsy

Lord, thank you. I have felt the grace of your presence continuously throughout this project. I have sensed your pleasure that this book was being written.

Heartfelt thanks to my birth mother, Virginia. You sacrificed to place me for adoption when your heart wanted to keep me. You are a hero.

And an eternity of gratitude to my wonderful adoptive parents, Lewis and Betty Schenck, who took a risk on me; loved me with a steadfast love; filled my life with fun, security, and opportunity; and grounded me in the Word of God and the reality of the Holy Spirit. I look forward to sharing the wonders of heaven with you.

Thank you, Chester, my husband, my delight and my partner in life for almost half a century. It made all the difference when you said, "You can do this, sweetheart. I'll be there to back you up." My part could not have been completed without your loving support and wonderful editing!

I also thank the Lord for Chosen Books, for editor Jane Campbell who helped my husband and me years ago as *Biblical Healing and Deliverance* was being birthed and published, and for

David Sluka, who shepherded this book. David, your words of encouragement were a catalyst in my decision to write again.

I also want to thank my dear friend and Canadian "daughter" Patricia Bootsma for suggesting this book to me and to David Sluka. May you smile to yourself as you see people benefit from it.

Last, how can I thank you, Jodi and Lisa, for this remarkable journey we've been on together. As iron sharpens iron, we've come out with a better book because of each other. Thank you for so honestly sharing the richness and challenges of your own journeys and for your insight, your vulnerability, your faith, and your passion to help all of us in the world of adoption. Your lives have deeply touched mine.

And Jodi, special kudos for keeping us on the path, helping us so diplomatically to sort out issues, and faithfully communicating with Chosen. You are a gifted leader and wonderful woman.

Lisa, I appreciate your heartfelt transparency and gifted expression. Thanks also for challenging me to look beyond my perspective to our wider audience. So valuable.

From Lisa

Thank you to David Sluka of Chosen Books for inviting me to share my story of being a foster youth and birth/first mom. It's uncommon for birth parents to be included in the conversation, and I appreciate the opportunity you gave me.

Jodi and Betsy, thank you for laboring with me on this project. We've created something together that we couldn't have done alone. What a treasure to call you my sisters in Christ.

To my parents, you loved me and did your best for me under extreme stress, thank you. As a mom of many kids, I know full well that we're all doing the best we can. I love you.

To my foster mom, who lived this story by my side, you have my deepest thanks.

Birth/first parents, your stories are often overlooked, yet your voices and experiences are crucial to a more complete understanding of adoption. Thank you to so many who have shared your stories with me.

To all my children, you fill my heart with love, and I am so thankful to be your mom.

I can hardly express my thanks to my husband, Russ, who grieved with me and helped me heal over our many years together. It required more of you than either of us ever imagined. Years later, you opened your heart and our home to Nick. You chose love when it wasn't easy.

Most of all, thank you to Jesus, who continues to write my life story in unexpected ways. You filled my arms with many children and now with grandchildren. I am nearly speechless with gratitude.

From Jodi

I want to begin by thanking my husband, Jerry, who gets far less credit than he deserves. Since the day we met unexpectedly, you have encouraged my every endeavor. With grace and patience, you led me into a deeper walk with God and discipled me with love and wisdom. Your "yes" made our complex and challenging life a great adventure. You really deserve all the accolades for always running by my side as I chase after God.

It's impossible to thank my children sufficiently for being my teachers. I don't know who I would be without you. I'm so grateful that you have always allowed your stories to be a hope and beacon for others.

I have the best friends in the world, and some of them were cheering me through every page of this book. I especially want to thank Deborah Janicke, Claudia Fletcher, and Anita Deyneka, all second mothers and writers, for telling me this book was important and for reading it and improving it so much along the way.

I'm immensely grateful to Betsy Kylstra, who had the opportunity to write this book and graciously invited me into it. What a gift that has been and what a gift you have been to my life. And I'm grateful to Lisa Qualls for bravely accepting our offer to be the birth mother voice.

David Sluka at Chosen, God gave you a burden for the healing of adoptive parents, and you made the commitment to birth this book. Thank you for your obedience and vision.

To the community of Second Mothers that surrounds me with love and upholds me when the light gets dim, you are my sisters on this journey, and I don't want to walk this road without you.

I am overwhelmingly grateful beyond words to our heavenly Father, who has made my life a beautiful tapestry beyond anything I could ever hope or imagine.

From the Authors

We wish to express our deepest gratitude to the birth parents, adoptees, and siblings who contributed their stories to this book. Your testimonies and courage are an inspiration.

NOTES

Chapter 1 Beginning with Hope

1. You can learn more about this ministry at RestoringTheFoundations.org.

Part One Acknowledging the Brokenness

1. I. W. R. Bushneil, F. Sai, and J. T. Mullin, "Neonatal Recognition of the Mother's Face," *British Journal of Developmental Psychology* 7, no. 1 (March 1989): 3–15, https://doi.org/10.1111/j.2044-835X.1989.tb00784.x; William P. Fifer, "The Fetus, the Newborn, and the Mother's Voice," in *The Infant and the Family in the Twenty-First Century*, ed. João Gomes-Pedro, J. Kevin Nugent, J. Gerald Young, and T. Berry Brazelton (New York: Brunner-Routledge, 2002), 79–85; Richard H. Porter, Jan Winberg, and Heidi Varendi, "Prenatal Preparation for Early Postnatal Olfactory Learning" in *Prenatal Development of Postnatal Functions*, ed. Brian Hopkins and Scott P. Johnson (Westport, CT: Praeger, 2005), 103–129.

2. Anver Siddiqui, Martin Eisemann, and Bruno Hägglöf, "The Stability of Maternal Interpretation of Infant's Facial Expressions During Pre- and Postnatal Period and Its Relation to Prenatal Attachment," *Early Child Development and Care* 162, no. 1 (2000): 41–50, https://doi.org/10.1080/0300443001620104.

3. Karyn Purvis and Lisa Qualls, *The Connected Parent: Real-Life Strategies for Building Trust and Attachment* (Eugene, OR: Harvest House Publishers, 2020), 36.

4. Purvis and Qualls, *The Connected Parent*, 36.

5. Purvis and Qualls, *The Connected Parent*, 37.

6. Bruce D. Perry and Maia Szalavitz, *The Boy Who Was Raised as a Dog and Other Stories from a Child Psychiatrist's Notebook: What Traumatized Children Can Teach Us about Loss, Love, and Healing* (New York: Basic Books, 2017), 258.

7. Bruce D. Perry and Oprah Winfrey, *What Happened to You: Conversations on Trauma, Resilience, and Healing* (New York: Flatiron Books, 2021), 108.

Chapter 2 Abandonment

1. Lisa Qualls and Karyn Purvis, *The Connected Parent: Real-Life Strategies for Building Trust and Attachment* (Eugene, OR: Harvest House Publishers, 2020).

2. Chester and Betsy Kylstra, *Biblical Healing and Deliverance* (Minneapolis: Chosen Books, 2014), 115.

3. Deuteronomy 31:6, Joshua 1:5, and Hebrews 13:5 are examples of this promise. This promise is also expressed throughout the Bible in many different ways.

4. Psalm 139:13 and Jeremiah 29:11.

Chapter 3 Grief and Loss

1. Lisa S. Zoll, LCSW, "Disenfranchised Grief: When Grief and Grievers Are Unrecognized," *The New Social Worker* 26, no. 1 (Winter 2019), https://www.social worker.com/feature-articles/practice/disenfranchised-grief-when-grief-and -grievers-are-unrecogniz.

2. Pauline Boss, *Ambiguous Loss: Learning to Live with Unresolved Grief* (Cambridge, MA: Harvard University Press, 2000).

3. Adapted from Betsy Kylstra, *Twice Chosen* (Nashville: Restoring The Foundations Publishing, 1996), 18–19. Used by permission.

Chapter 4 Shame and Isolation

1. Edward T. Welch, *Shame Interrupted: How God Lifts the Pain of Worthlessness and Rejection* (Greensboro, NC: New Growth Press, 2012), 2.

2. Chester and Betsy Kylstra, *Biblical Healing and Deliverance* (Minneapolis: Chosen Books, 2014), ch. 3.

3. Kylstra and Kylstra, *Biblical Healing and Deliverance*, 99–101.

4. Adapted from Chester and Betsy Kylstra, "My Story Questionnaire" (application for ministry, Restoring The Foundations), updated April 10, 2023, page 8, https://my.restoringthefoundations.org/documents/my-story.

5. Adapted from Chester and Betsy Kylstra, *Shame, Fear, Control* MP3 audio (Nashville: Restoring The Foundations Publishing, 2000).

Chapter 6 Facing the Unknown

1. *Oxford English Dictionary*, s.v. "lament," accessed January 17, 2024, https://www.oed.com/search/dictionary/?scope=Entries&q=lament.

2. *Merriam-Webster*, s.v. "lament," accessed January 17, 2024, https://www.merriam -webster.com/dictionary/lament.

3. Mark Vroegop, *Dark Clouds, Deep Mercy: Discovering the Grace of Lament* (Wheaton, IL: Crossway, 2019), 28.

4. Vroegop, *Dark Clouds, Deep Mercy*, 35.

Chapter 7 Truth and Lies about You

1. The original author of this saying is unknown.

2. Thomas Verny with John Kelly, *The Secret Life of the Unborn Child: How You Can Prepare Your Baby for a Happy, Healthy Life* (New York: Dell Publishing, 1982).

Chapter 8 Hurts and Wounds

1. Adapted from Betsy Kylstra, *Twice Chosen* (Nashville: Restoring The Foundations Publishing, 1996), 91–92. Used by permission.

Chapter 9 Defeating the Enemy

1. Chester and Betsy Kylstra, *Biblical Healing and Deliverance* (Minneapolis: Chosen Books, 2014), ch. 6.
2. CSB.
3. CSB.

Chapter 10 Forgiveness

1. John Arnott and Carol Arnott, *Grace and Forgiveness: A Powerful Key to Your Freedom and Healing* (Shippensburg, PA: Destiny Image Publishers, 2022).
2. Chester and Betsy Kylstra and Dorathy Railey, *Restoring the Foundations Ministry Tools* (Nashville: Restoring The Foundations Publishing, 2016).
3. KJV.

Part Three Experiencing Wholeness

1. Quote attributed to Mother Teresa in *Something Beautiful for God* (San Francisco: Harper One, 2003).

Chapter 11 Redemption and Life in Christ

1. If you'd like to experience more of the Father's love, we recommend *Finding Father*, a video course by Alyn and AJ Jones that can be obtained at AlynAndAJ.com.

Chapter 12 Going Deeper in Healing Prayer

1. Many of the Healing House Network ministers at Restoring The Foundations International are specifically trained in this area. Please ask for one with these qualifications. RestoringTheFoundations.org
2. Steve and Barbara Chua, *Free to Be Me: Unlocking All You Were Created to Be* (Claremont, CA: Steve Chua International, 2023), 101.
3. Chester and Betsy Kylstra, *Biblical Healing and Deliverance* (Minneapolis: Chosen Books, 2014), 57–92.
4. Adapted from Chester and Betsy Kylstra, "Ministry Card" (Restoring The Foundations), 2003.
5. Adapted from Kylstra and Kylstra, "Ministry Card."
6. Job 22:28.
7. Adapted from Kylstra and Kylstra, "Ministry Card."
8. Many of the Healing House Network ministers at Restoring The Foundations International are specifically trained in this area. Please ask for one with these qualifications. www.RestoringTheFoundations.org
9. Kylstra and Kylstra, *Biblical Healing and Deliverance*, ch. 6.
10. Adapted from Kylstra and Kylstra, "Ministry Card."

HELPFUL RESOURCES

Second Mothers community and resources: SecondMothers .com, on Facebook @SecondMothers, and YouTube @Second Mother. Also join a private support group at Facebook.com /groups/SecondMother.

Compassionate support and soul care for adoptive/foster/ kinship moms: Join The Hope Circle at Facebook.com/groups /OneThankfulMom. Find information about Lisa's writing, speaking, coaching, and retreats at LisaCQualls.com.

Restoring The Foundations International Ministry: Go to RestoringTheFoundations.org to learn details of the RTF revelation, how to receive God's healing, and how to receive ministry from an RTF Healing House Ministry team.

Other Related Books by These Authors

The Connected Parent: Real-Life Strategies for Building Trust and Attachment by Karyn Purvis and Lisa C. Qualls

Reclaim Compassion: The Adoptive Parent's Guide to Overcoming Blocked Care with Neuroscience and Faith by Lisa C. Qualls and Melissa Corkum

Second Mother: A Bible Study Experience for Foster and Adoptive Moms by Jodi Jackson Tucker

Fasten Your Sweet Belt: 10 Things You Need to Know about Older Child Adoption by Jodi Jackson Tucker with Agnes Tucker

Restoring the Foundations: An Integrated Approach to Healing Ministry by Chester and Betsy Kylstra

Biblical Healing and Deliverance: A Guide to Experiencing Freedom from Sins of the Past, Destructive Beliefs, Emotional and Spiritual Pain, Curses, and Oppression by Chester and Betsy Kylstra

Would You Be Willing?: The Story of Restoring the Foundations at Echo Mountain Inn by Chester and Betsy Kylstra

Twice Chosen: One Woman's Story of Healing by Betsy Kylstra

Resources to Learn about Hearing God's Voice

4 Keys to Hearing God's Voice by Mark and Patti Virkler

Translating God: Hearing God's Voice for Yourself and the World Around You by Shawn Bolz

Born to an unwed teenager, **Betsy S. Kylstra** was soon adopted by loving, wise parents. Even with many advantages, however, she experienced the deep pain and struggles common to many adoptees. Betsy's Christian upbringing, plus her healing encounters with God, led to the healing of her heart and also launched her into co-founding with her husband Restoring The Foundations International, a ministry providing healing to individuals and couples. Betsy's three advanced degrees include a master's in biblical studies. She is coauthor of *Restoring the Foundations* and *Biblical Healing and Deliverance* as well as other books. She and her husband, Chester, have four adult children and four grandchildren.

Connect with Betsy:

 PHW.org

 RestoringTheFoundations.org

As a birth mom, former foster youth, foster mom, and adoptive mom, **Lisa C. Qualls** provides insight and resources to parents and professionals through speaking, writing, and coaching. Lisa is a Trust-Based Relational Intervention (TBRI®) practitioner, Christian spiritual director, parent coach, and cofounder of Adoption Wise. She is also the coauthor of *The Connected Parent: Real-Life Strategies for Building Trust and Attachment* (with Dr. Karyn Purvis) and coauthor of *Reclaim Compassion: The Adoptive Parent's Guide to Overcoming Blocked Care with Neuroscience and Faith* (with Melissa Corkum). Lisa lives in North Idaho with her husband, Russ. They have twelve children by birth and adoption and two beautiful granddaughters.

Connect with Lisa:

 LisaCQualls.com

 @LisaCQualls

 @OneThankfulMom

A passionate advocate for the family, **Jodi Jackson Tucker** leads Second Mothers, a community for foster and adoptive parents. Second Mothers offers events, an online support group, a video channel, and global relief to vulnerable mothers and children in crisis. Jodi previously served as the global director of Orphan Sunday for the Christian Alliance for Orphans, where she led its expansion to more than ninety nations. She is the author of *Second Mother: A Bible Study Experience for Foster and Adoptive Moms* and *Fasten Your Sweet Belt: 10 Things You Need to Know about Older Child Adoption*. Jodi is a seminary graduate and certified chaplain. She and her husband, Jerry, are parents of eight adult children, five through domestic and international adoption.

Connect with Jodi:

 JodiJacksonTucker.com and SecondMothers.org

 @SecondMothers and @groups/SecondMother

 @SecondMother